Advanced Excel Essentials

Jordan Goldmeier

Advanced Excel Essentials

ISBN-13 (pbk): 978-1-4842-0735-2

ISBN-13 (electronic): 978-1-4842-0734-5

Managing Director: Welmoed Spahr
Lead Editor: James DeWolf
Technical Reviewer: Fabio Ferracchiati
Editorial Board: Steve Anglin, Mark Beckner, Ewan Buckingham, Gary Cornell, Louise Corrigan, Jim DeWolf, Jonathan Gennick, Robert Hutchinson, Michelle Lowman, James Markham, Matthew Moodie, Jeff Olson, Jeffrey Pepper, Douglas Pundick, Ben Renow-Clarke, Dominic Shakeshaft, Gwenan Spearing, Matt Wade, Steve Weiss
Coordinating Editor: Kevin Walter
Copy Editor: Mary Behr
Compositor: SPi Global
Indexer: SPi Global
Artist: SPi Global
Cover Designer: Anna Ishchenko

Distributed to the book trade worldwide by Springer Science+Business Media New York, 233 Spring Street, 6th Floor, New York, NY 10013. Phone 1-800-SPRINGER, fax (201) 348-4505, e-mail orders-ny@springer-sbm.com, or visit www.springeronline.com. Apress Media, LLC is a California LLC and the sole member (owner) is Springer Science + Business Media Finance Inc (SSBM Finance Inc). SSBM Finance Inc is a Delaware corporation.

For information on translations, please e-mail rights@apress.com, or visit www.apress.com.

Apress and friends of ED books may be purchased in bulk for academic, corporate, or promotional use. eBook versions and licenses are also available for most titles. For more information, reference our Special Bulk Sales–eBook Licensing web page at www.apress.com/bulk-sales.

Any source code or other supplementary material referenced by the author in this text is available to readers at www.apress.com. For detailed information about how to locate your book's source code, go to www.apress.com/source-code/.

Dedicated to my lovely wife, Katherine, who, as an undergrad, failed her required remedial Excel course three times

Contents at a Glance

Contents

About the Author

Jordan Goldmeier is a management consultant, author, educator, producer, and Microsoft MVP. He is the owner of Cambia Factor (www.cambiafactor.com), a data consulting agency, where he challenges companies and institutions to rethink how they collect, work with, and interpret data. He has provided spreadsheet-based decision support services to the NATO Training Mission in Afghanistan, the Pentagon, Navy, Air Force, and Army as well as training and consultation to private financial institutions in big data analytics and data visualization. Outside of work, Jordan is a producer for and host of Excel.TV, a web series dedicated to talking to and learning from Excel experts. Jordan also loves grilling, smoked meats, and all things BBQ. He lives in Dayton, Ohio with his wife.

About the Technical Reviewer

Fabio Claudio Ferracchiati is a senior consultant and a senior analyst/developer using Microsoft technologies. He works at BluArancio SpA (www.bluarancio.com) as Senior Analyst/Developer and Microsoft Dynamics CRM Specialist. He is a Microsoft Certified Solution Developer for .NET, a Microsoft Certified Application Developer for .NET, a Microsoft Certified Professional, and a prolific author and technical reviewer. Over the past ten years, he's written articles for Italian and international magazines and coauthored more than ten books on a variety of computer topics.

Acknowledgments

I'm not good at writing these sections. There are simply too many people to thank and acknowledge. So, before anything else, let me first acknowledge *everyone* who has ever talked to me about Excel over the last five years of my life. You know who you are. You played a key role in the formation of this book. You argued with me about using `Option Explicit`, helping me establish why I believed using it is so important. You proposed alternate solutions to methods I never questioned. This book is as much yours as it is mine. In fact, feel free to write your name with mine on the first page of the book. You've earned it.

If I'm being honest, this book was really lead editor Jim DeWolfe's brilliant idea. Sure, I wrote it, but it would have never happened without him. If there's any sense of organization or elegance in my writing, it's surely due to developmental editor, Chris Nelson, whose ability to spin rambling thoughts into coherent ideas is nothing short of editorial alchemy. There's also Fabio Claudio Ferracchiati, my technical editor, whose words of encouragement were proof that I was writing something worth reading. And, Mary Behr, my copyeditor, who had the unenviable task of trimming up my loquacious writing. Also, Kevin Walter, my coordinating editor, who kept us all on track. Finally, let's not forget the entire Apress editorial team, who graciously allowed me to publish an `additional` book when I was so very behind on my first for them.

There are also several individuals who, whether they realize it or not, have made profound contributions to this book (and to my work, in general). In no specific order, I'd like to thank and acknowledge Alex Gutman, Purna "Chandoo" Duggirala, Daniel Ferry, Krisztina Szabó, Roberto Mensa, Robert Mundigl, Cary Walkin, Dick Kusleika, Bill "MrExcel" Jelen, Szilvia Juhasz, Rick Grantham, Oz du Soleil, Rahim Zulfiqar Ali, and Jeff Weir.

Of course, there's no way I could have completed this book without the love and support of my wife, Katherine (who has been working on finishing her PhD and dissertation in addition to putting up with me writing all the time). Whenever I felt stuck in my writing, she encouraged me to push through. And then there's my brother, Stephen, who has always been a tireless champion of my work.

The reason I even thought I could write a book was because of the support and feedback from the Excel community. The Excel community has some of the finest talent in the world working to solve problems with Excel nobody thought possible. This book is only but a small contribution to the work of the entire community.

Finally, I can't forget to acknowledge Google Spreadsheets for all the great work it has done converting people back to Excel.

PART I

■ ■ ■

Core Advanced Excel Concepts

In this part, I'll review the core concepts that make up the essentials of advanced Excel.

Chapter 1 explains what is meant by advanced Excel development, and how this book differs from many others. For instance, several books place significant emphasis on Visual Basic for Applications code, believing macros to be the most important feature of Excel development. This chapter will challenge that notion and present advanced concepts as a product of many different Excel features, including code. Additionally, I discuss the most important required skill—creativity.

Chapter 2 provides a brief Visual Basic for Applications refresher. I'll discuss how best to set up the coding environment to make it conducive to headache-free coding. I'll also challenge conventional coding conventions and propose alternatives that will prove more effective.

Chapter 3 introduces the formula concepts that will be used in this book. The chapter starts with tips that will make your experience developing advanced formulas run more smoothly. I'll then show you how to perform advanced calculations by simply using range operators. You'll develop advanced alternatives to the IF function that will prove more powerful in practice and more readable later on. In addition, you'll investigate the full extent of Excel's Boolean logic features.

Chapter 4 continues the discussion of formulas by demonstrating how they can be used with advanced applications. I take you through several examples applying these formula concepts and demonstrate how they can be understood with a little bit of algebra. The chapter concludes by introducing the notion of reusable components, which are spreadsheet mechanics that can be easily reused for other projects.

Chapter 5 shows how advanced capabilities can be built into spreadsheets by using the humble form control. In this chapter, I argue against using ActiveX and UserForms. Instead, you'll rely on the flexibility of form controls combined with the speed and prowess of formulas. Chapter 5 concludes with several practical reusable components that you can start using in your own work right away.

■ ■ ■

CHAPTER 1

Introduction to Advanced Excel Essentials

I set out to write a book on the *essentials* of Excel development—that is, a book that concisely presents many of the development principles and practices I've discovered through my work and consulting experience.

But whether on purpose or by accident, this book has become something considerably more than that. Indeed, another name for this book could be *A Contrarian's Guide To Excel Development*. You see, this book will push back against the wisdom of other terrific Excel books, including my favorite book, *Professional Excel Development* (Addison-Wesley 2005). To be sure, the information in those books is terrific, and whatever merits this book might achieve, it will likely never come close to the impact of *Professional Excel Development*.

At the same time, much of the information in these books, I believe, is somewhat dated. For instance, let's take the case of Hungarian Notation. Hungarian Notation is a variable naming convention encouraged by virtually all Excel development books. Even if you've never heard of Hungarian Notation, you've likely seen and used it, if you've ever looked at or learned from example code. It basically says a variable's name should start with a prefix of the variable's type. For instance, lblCaption, intCounter, and strTitle are all examples of Hungarian Notation: the lbl in lblCaption tells us we're working with a Label object; the int in intCounter tells us we're working with an integer type, and the str in strTitle tell us we're working with a string type. If you've done any VBA coding before, this is likely not new information.

You might not know this, however: most modern languages have all but abandoned Hungarian Notation. Microsoft's .NET style guidelines, for instance, even discourage its use. More than a decade has passed since Microsoft last recommended Hungarian Notation. I argue that it's time for a more modern naming style, which I introduce in Chapter 2.

But this book is concerned with more than just naming conventions. I argue that we should change the way we think about development. Previous books have placed significant emphasis on user interface with ActiveX objects and UserForms. This book will eschew these bloated controls; rather, this book will show you how to develop complex interactivity using the spreadsheet as your canvas. You'll see that it's easier and provides for more control and flexibility compared to conventional methods from other books.

In addition, I'll place less emphasis on code and a stronger emphasis on formulas (Chapters 3, 4, and 5). Many books have narrowly defined the principles of advanced Excel in terms of VBA code. But formulas can be powerful. And often they can be used in place of VBA code. You might be surprised by how much interactivity you can create without writing a single line of code. And how much quicker your spreadsheet runs because of it.

This book is divided into two parts. Part I (Chapters 1-5) deals with concepts that are likely already familiar to you. Specifically they concern VBA code and formulas—but I present these concepts in new ways. Part II makes up the last four chapters of the book (Chapters 6-9). These chapters apply concepts from Part I to a real-world example product I built in my consulting experience. Futhermore, in Part II, you'll learn how to input form data without making your spreadsheet bloated. You'll also apply some data analytics used in the field of management science.

However, if you learn anything from my book, it should be that the process of development never stops. The most important skill you'll need is creativity. Just as I saw different ways to approach a problem than my predecessors, so too should you analyze what's being presented to you. Undoubtedly, you'll find even better approaches than I did. I don't expect everyone to agree with my approaches, but what's important is that you understand them, so you can see what works, what doesn't, and why. Because you won't become an advanced Excel developer through rote memorization of the material presented herein; you must learn to think like an advanced developer. This book will teach you the essentials of doing just that.

What to Expect from this Book

This is not a beginner level book. I assume you have intermediate level experience with formulas and Visual Basic for Applications. At the very least, you should be able to understand and write both formulas and code. Complete mastery isn't necessary; because the topics presented in this book are somewhat new, a mastery in these topics might not even help you. All that being said, if you're an experienced Excel user—and you have the aptitude and thirst to learn new things—there's no reason you won't be successful in reading this book! Again, the most important (and cherished) skill that will guarantee your success is creativity.

What's considered "advanced" may mean different things to different people. Here, we're interested in the principles that help us become better spreadsheet users and developers. That said, this book will make use of Excel features such as formulas, tables, conditional formatting, Visual Basic for Applications code, form controls, and charts. For the most part, I will present a brief refresher on what these features do and how they are used. However, you'll find this book moves at a quicker pace than beginner level treatments for these items. Features such as PivotTables, PowerPivot, Power Map, and data tables are not discussed in this book. But you'll find that the principles presented in these pages are extendable to these topics.

Indeed, this book is most concerned with teaching Excel development as first principles. I will explain what they are and how best they are used in practice. Once you learn underlying concepts, extending their use into applications becomes trivial.

Example Files Used in This Book

This book comes with many examples as a complement to the material presented herein. The example files are organized by chapter. Whenever there is a corresponding example file for the material presented, I'll provide you the name of the example file in the text. All example files are freely available to download from the book's Apress web page (www.apress.com/9781484207352). The files are designed to work in Excel 2007 and newer.

The Two Most Important Principles

There are many different ideas and concepts presented in this book. But I'll be daring and attempt to sum them up as two key concepts:

1. When it make sense, do more with less.

2. Break every rule.

■ **Note** The two most important principles are (1) when it makes sense, do more with less, and (2) break every rule.

When It Makes Sense, Do More with Less

You don't need VBA to do everything. Many times, the reason a spreadsheet is slow is because there is too much reliance on code. Similarly, too many formulas—especially volatile functions like OFFSET and INDIRECT—will almost always slow down a spreadsheet. There are better alternatives to these methods. Often, they require less code and can get more done.

However, we should be wary of brevity for the sake of it. Bill "MrExcel" Jelen and I have a friendly disagreement[1] on whether to use Option Explicit in your code. He says he doesn't need it because he always writes perfect code to start with—and that its use needlessly adds more lines of code. I, of course, respectfully disagree. I strongly encourage you to use Option Explicit. Option Explicit requires that you declare your variables before they're used. That means that you cannot introduce a new variable in your code on the fly. Listing 1-1 shows code without Option Explicit; Listing 1-2 shows code with Option Explicit.

Listing 1-1. No Option Explicit

```
Public Sub MyResponse()
    ResponseMessage = "Code Executed Successfully!"
    MsgBox ResponseMessage
End Sub
```

Listing 1-2. With Option Explicit

```
Option Explicit

Public Sub MyResponse()
    Dim ResponseMessage as String

    ResponseMessage = "Code Executed Successfully!"
    MsgBox ResponseMessage
End Sub
```

Bill argued using Option Explicit required at least one additional line of code for every variable. And it might appear Listing 1-1 is indeed doing more (or at least *the same*) with less code. But, as I show in Chapter 2, not using Option Explicit might be more trouble than it is worth. Debugging is much harder without Option Explicit, and not using it even encourages sloppy code. From my standpoint, leaving out Option Explicit (and the required variable declaration) is simply getting less done with less code. But however you feel on this particular issue, it's worth testing your opinion against that first principle: ask yourself, am I really doing more with less?

Break Every Rule

I truly believe, and stand by, the material presented in this book. But I would have never discovered any of it without departing from conventional wisdom. Again, I'll keep hammering this point until I am blue in the face: the most important takeaway from this book is creativity. And you cannot be creative without pushing a few boundaries. Don't be scared to crash a spreadsheet or two in the pursuit of learning.

You'll see in later chapters that some techniques won't always be the best choice for every scenario. For instance, a complex formula that is much faster in practice than a conventional formula might be useless if you must share your spreadsheet and you're the only one who understands it. There will always be an economy between formula readability and utility. I present complex formulas in this book, but I also argue that readability should be a factor in choosing when and where to use them.

---

[1]Watch Bill and I fight about this on Excel.TV: www.youtube.com/watch?v=yJRLzN3Dzmw.

Most important, you shouldn't be satisfied with Excel's perceived limitations. Over the last several years, I've been blown away by what I've seen others accomplish with Excel. There is a thriving online community dedicated to helping people realize their imaginations with spreadsheets. Whenever I need inspiration, I look to the community.

For your own consideration, I'll provide two examples of my own work that show what can be done with Excel when we think creatively. Figure 1-1 shows a three dimensional maze I created. It might surprise you to learn there is very little code involved. And the "maze" is simply an area chart formatted to look like a three dimensional plane.

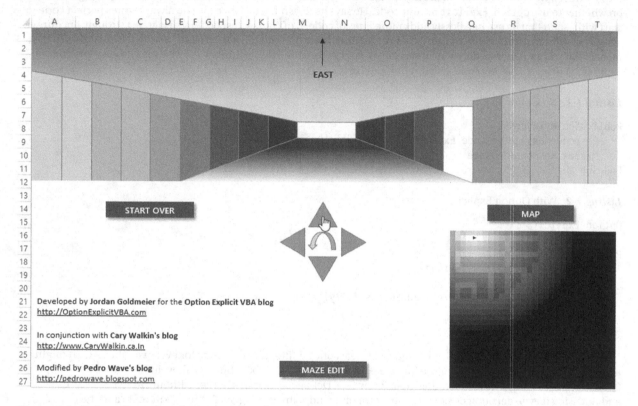

Figure 1-1. A three dimensional maze, made with Excel

The second item I would like to present is a periodic table of elements with Excel, shown in Figure 1-2. The periodic table uses a mouseover capability. When the user hovers their mouse over a cell, a macro is executed that updates information about the element. However, the macro uses only a few lines of code, and besides that update, the functionality is largely driven by formula functions. Moreover, that mouseover capability is one I discovered by accident. Before I first wrote about it on my blog, it had been considered impossible.

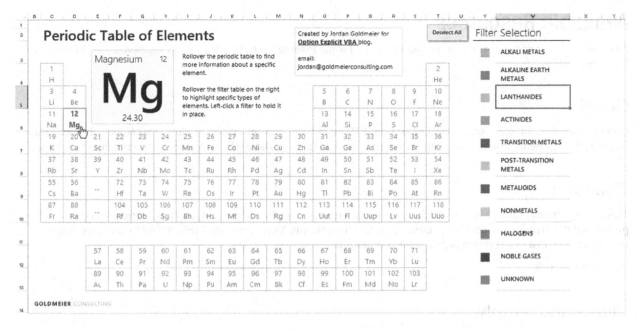

Figure 1-2. *A periodic table of elements with interactivty previously thought impossible with Excel*

Both the three dimensional maze and periodic table are available for you to investigate in the project files included with this book. While it's beyond the scope of this book to explain in detail how these particular spreadsheets were created, they are the direct product of the material I present in the rest of the book. However, if you're interested in reading how these items were developed, see the links in the sidebar.

LINKS ON DEVELOPING A MAZE AND MOUSE OVER MECHANISM

How to Create a Rollover Effect in Excel: Execute a Macro When Your Mouse is Over a Cell

http://optionexplicitvba.blogspot.com/2011/04/rollover-b8-ov1.html

Roll Over Tooltips and Web Actions on a Microsoft Excel Dashboard

www.clearlyandsimply.com/clearly_and_simply/2012/11/roll-over-tooltips-and-web-actions-on-a-microsoft-excel-dashboard.html

Development Principles for Excel Games and Applications

http://optionexplicitvba.com/2013/09/16/development-principles-for-excel-games-and-applications/

Your First Maze

http://optionexplicitvba.com/2013/09/17/your-first-maze-2/

Available Resources

As I said in the previous section, sometimes you need some inspiration to help get you going. Here's a list of resources I use regularly.

Google

Google...Google...Google! Google is your best friend. If you're ever stuck on a problem, simply ask Google the same way you might your friend. Usually, you'll find the results in Excel forums where folks have asked the very same questions.

Chandoo

This site, by Purna "Chandoo" Duggirala, is a phenomenal resource for every Excel developer, from novice to professional. Chandoo covers many topics including dashboards, VBA, data visualization, and formula techniques. His site is also host to a thriving online forum community.

www.chandoo.org

Cleary and Simply

Clearly and Simply is a site by Robert Mundigl. The site is mainly focused on dashboards and data visualization techniques with Excel and Tableau.

www.ClearlyAndSimply.com

Contextures

Debra Dalgleish runs the Contextures web site, which focuses on Excel development and dashboards, particularly with PivotTables. Her approach to dashboards and the use of PivotTables is different from mine, but well worth a read. She is also the author of these Apress Books:

- *Excel Pivot Tables Recipe Book: A Problem-Solution Approach*
- *Beginning PivotTables in Excel 2007: From Novice to Professional*

www.contextures.com

Excel Hero

Excel Hero was created by Daniel Ferry. While his blog is not very active anymore, you will find his older content incredibly useful. Several of his articles have served as the inspiration for the content found in these pages.

www.ExcelHero.com

Peltier Tech

Jon Peltier is a chartmaster. His web site is full of charting tutorials and examples. He provides sage wisdom on data visualization and proper data analysis. His web site covers every conceivable thing you might want to do with a chart in Excel.

www.peltiertech.com

The Last Word

Above all, advanced development is about thinking creatively. You'll see this in practice in the chapters to come. Because some of the material is new, it may appear challenging at first. You may even find yourself frustrated at times. In these moments, it's best to take a break for a moment, find your bearings, and start from the beginning of the section in which you left off. The material is complex, but well within your grasp. I urge you to push through to the end of the book. The material is worth it; but more important, you're worth it. What will you learn in this book will distinguish you. We're only still scratching the surface of what Excel can do. By the time you're finished with this book, you'll be developing work that might even surprise you.

CHAPTER 2

■ ■ ■

Visual Basic for Applications for Excel, a Refresher

Of course, no advanced book on developing anything in Excel would be complete without a chapter on the interpreter language housed within Excel, Visual Basic for Applications–or better known by its shorthand moniker, VBA.

This chapter won't be an introduction to VBA but rather a review of VBA programming techniques and development principles found in this book and practiced throughout most of my career. What follows may appear unconventional, at first. Indeed, it may differ somewhat from what you've been previously taught. However, I don't leave you with a few instructions and no guidance. Instead, I'll explain in detail why I believe what I believe—and why you should believe as I do. If you find that you don't—and I certainly welcome disagreement—consider the other important—actually, more important—takeaway from this chapter: the code choices and styles we use should always follow from a set of principles, guidelines, and convention. When you code, do so with structure and meaning. Know *why* you believe what you believe.

But, the most important thing to do right now is to ready yourself to begin coding. This requires that you set the right conditions in your coding environment.

Making the Most of Your Coding Experience

I tend to get more done when I'm less frustrated. I'll be so daring to suggest you're probably the same way. And let's not kid ourselves: coding in VBA can be a frustrating experience. For instance, have you ever been halfway through writing an IF statement and then realized you needed to fix something on another line? So you click that other line and Excel stops everything to pop up a message box saying that you've written a syntax error, like in Figure 2-1. Chances are, you already knew that. In fact, you wanted to change an earlier line in the code to prevent another error from happening.

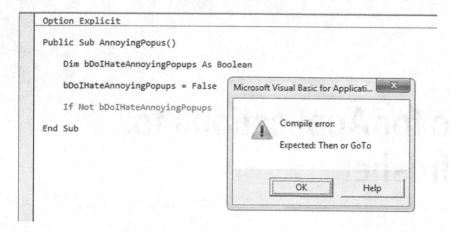

```
Option Explicit

Public Sub AnnoyingPopus()

    Dim bDoIHateAnnoyingPopups As Boolean

    bDoIHateAnnoyingPopups = False

    If Not bDoIHateAnnoyingPopups

End Sub
```

Microsoft Visual Basic for Applicati...

⚠ Compile error:

Expected: Then or GoTo

[OK]   [Help]

Figure 2-1. *That all-too-annoying popup error box telling you what you likely already know*

Tell Excel: Stop Annoying Me!

I mean, nobody's perfect, but you don't need this popup ruining your coding flow every time you click to another line. So, save yourself from unnecessary popups by disabling Auto Syntax Check from the Options dialog box, which you access by selecting Tools > Options (see Figure 2-2). This will only disable the popup. The offending syntax error is still highlighted in red—in other words, you don't lose any functionality, just the annoyance.

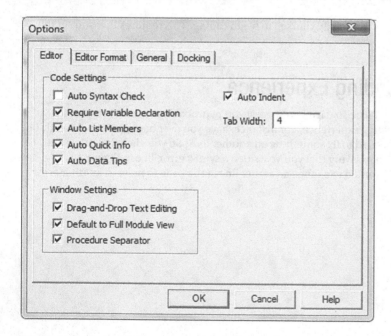

Figure 2-2. *Uncheck Auto Syntax Check for distraction-free coding*

Make Loud Comments

If you comment your code regularly—and you should—you've probably noticed comments don't "stand out" very much. In fact, I'll be the first to admit I've gone through code and missed comments because they've "blended in" with their surroundings. Figure 2-3 shows perhaps a more extreme example involving rather busy code, but the point remains: the two comment markers (') I've placed in the routine are not easily or immediately found.

```
Public Sub CommentTest()
    MsgBox "1"
    MsgBox "2            "
    MsgBox "3       "
    MsgBox "4                "
    MsgBox "          5    "
    MsgBox "6    "  '
    MsgBox "      7    "
    MsgBox "        8   "
    MsgBox "                9   "
    MsgBox "    10   "
    MsgBox "        11    "
    MsgBox "         12    "
    MsgBox "14        "  '
    MsgBox "     15    "
    MsgBox "16    "
End Sub
```

Figure 2-3. *Comment markers at 6 and 14 blend in with the code*

Luckily, you don't have to use the preset colors. In fact, you can make the comments stand out. Go back to the Options dialog box from the Tools menu. Click the Editor Format tab and select Comment Text from the Code Colors list box. Below the list box you can specify the foreground and background color, which are the text color and highlight properties, respectively (see Figure 2-4). Personally, I like using a dark blue foreground and light blue background (see Figure 2-5). You'll have to try this on your own to get the full effect; to that end, and to preserve the formatting guidelines of this book, the highlight does not appear in the code listings throughout the book.

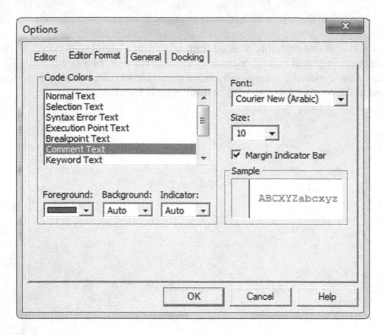

Figure 2-4. *The Editor Format dialog box*

```
Public Sub CommentTest()
    MsgBox "1"
    MsgBox "2          "
    MsgBox "3      "
    MsgBox "4              "
    MsgBox "        5   "
    MsgBox "6    " 
    MsgBox "      7   "
    MsgBox "        8   "
    MsgBox "             9    "
    MsgBox "   10    "
    MsgBox "      11    "
    MsgBox "        12    "
    MsgBox "14       " 
    MsgBox "     15    "
    MsgBox "16    "
End Sub
```

Figure 2-5. *Let your comments be heard with bold colors*

Pick a Readable Font

Leave that Options dialog box open because you'll need it once more. By default, Excel uses Courier New (Figure 2-6) as its default coding font. Again, this font, like the comment style defaults, doesn't emphasizes the clear readability. I prefer the font Consolas shown in Figure 2-7 because I think it does a much a better job in this regard.

```
Option Explicit

Public Sub CommentTest()
    MsgBox "Try Reading this Font."
End Sub
```

Figure 2-6. *Sample code with Courier New as the font*

```
Option Explicit

Public Sub CommentTest()
    MsgBox "Try Reading this Font."
End Sub
```

Figure 2-7. *More readable text with Consolas*

You can change the font by selecting Normal Text from the list box (Figure 2-4) and using the font dropdown on the side of the dialog box. Excel gives you lots of fonts to choose from, but the best fonts with which to code are those of fixed width. So if you choose something other than Consolas or Courier New, make sure to pick a readable, fixed-width font.

Start Using the Immediate Window, Immediately

The Immediate window is like a handy scratchpad with many uses. If the Immediate window is not already open, go to View ➤ Immediate Window in the Visual Basic Editor. You can type calculations and expressions directly into the Immediate window using the print keyword. Figure 2-8 provides some examples of typing directly into the Immediate window.

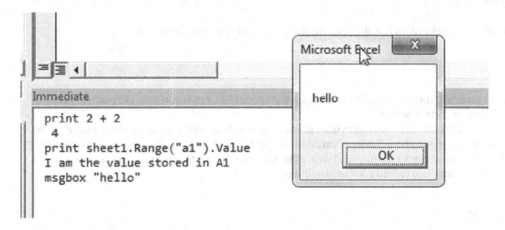

Figure 2-8. *The Immediate window*

15

In addition, you can also print the response of a loop or method directly into the Immediate window. To do this, use Debug.Print. Listing 2-1 shows you how.

Listing 2-1. Using Debug.Print to Write to the Immediate Window While in Runtime

```
For i = 1 to 100
    Debug.Print "Current Iteration: " & i
Next i
Debug.Print "Loop finished."
```

Opt for Option Explicit

VBA doesn't require you declare your variables before using them—that is, unless you place the words Option Explicit at the top of your code module. Without Option Explicit, the For loop from Listing 2-1 would run without problems. When you use Option Explicit, you must declare all variables before they are used. In Listing 2-2, I've used the Dim keyword to declare the integer i.

Listing 2-2. A For-Next Loop with Declared Variables

```
Dim i as Integer
For i = 1 to 100
    Debug.Print "Current Iteration: " & i
Next i
Debug.Print "Loop finished."
```

If you forgo Option Explicit, as I did in the first instance, Excel will simply create the variable i for you. However, that i won't be an integer; rather it will be of a *variant* type. This may not sound like such a bad thing at first, but letting Excel simply make variables for you is a recipe for trouble. What if you misspell a variable, like RecordCount, as I've done in Listing 2-3?

Listing 2-3. An Example of a Variable Created on the Spot Because Option Explicit Wasn't Used

```
RecordCount = 1
Msgbox RecordCout
```

Excel won't alert you to an error. Instead, it will simply create RecordCout as a new variable. Do you trust your ability to find misspellings in your code quickly?

In practice, I've found using Option Explicit alleviates many potential headaches. So do yourself a favor, in the Option dialog box (Tools ➤ Options), check Require Variable Declaration to Excel to automatically (and proudly) display Option Explicit at the top of every module. And when the error in Figure 2-9 appears, give yourself a pat on the back for not having to scour your code to find your misspellings.

Figure 2-9. *Breath a sigh of relief! You have Option Explicit on the case!*

Seriously, I can't tell you how important Option Explicit is. I'd repeat "Always use Option Explicit!" 1,000 times here if I could. But I'll just let Excel do it for me instead. Paste the following formula into an empty cell before moving to the next section.

```
=REPT("Always use Option Explicit! ",1000)
```

Naming Conventions

A naming convention is a common identification system for variables, constants, and objects. By definition, then, a good naming convention should be sufficiently descriptive about the content and nature of the thing named. In the next subsections, I'll talk about two naming conventions. The first, Hungarian Notation, is the most common notation used for VBA coding. Indeed, I'm unaware of any book that has argued against its use—that is, until now. The second, my preferred notation, is what I call "loose" CamelCase notation, and it's similar to the standard for just about all modern object-oriented languages.

Hungarian Notation

In this section, I'll talk about Hungarian Notation. In this notation, the variable name consists of a prefix—usually an abbreviated description the variable's type—followed by one or two words describing the variable's function (e.g. its reason for existing). For example, in Listing 2-4, the "s" before Title is used to indicate the variable is of String type. The term "title," as I'm sure you can guess, describes to the string's *function*—in other words, its reason for existing.

Listing 2-4. An Example of Hungarian Notation

```
Dim sTitle as String
sTitle = "The new spreadsheet.!"
```

Table 2-1 shows some suggested prefixes for common variables and classes.

Table 2-1. *Prefixes Suggested by Hungarian Notation*

Prefix	Data Type
B	Boolean
D	Double
I	Integer
S	String
V	Variant
Rng	Excel.Range
Obj	Excel.Object
Chrt	Excel.Chart
Ws	Excel.Worksheet
Wb	Excel.Workbook

In this book, I will discourage the use of Hungarian Notation in your code. I'm not here to tell you that Hungarian Notation is terrible because it does have its uses. For instance, VBA code isn't known for having very strict data type rules. This means you can assign integers to strings without casting from one type to the other. So including the type in a variables name isn't a terrible idea at all.

But much of this type confusion can be resolved by using descriptive and proper variables names, as you'll see in the next few pages. For now, however, it's a good idea to at least familiarize yourself with Hungarian Notation if you haven't done so already. Hungarian Notation is still widely used in VBA to this day, so it's important that you can read it proficiently even if you decide in this moment to never use it again. (Good choice!)

The fact is, Hungarian Notation is old. Indeed, in many ways, it's a relic of a bygone era–namely, the era in which people still used Visual Basic 6.0. (Those were the days, right?) In fact, Microsoft's Design Guidelines for .NET libraries has discouraged its use for more than decade. So what I'm proposing in this next section might feel new, but it's actually been around for quite some time.

"Loose" CamelCase Notation

In this section, I'll talk about loose CamelCase notation as my preferred alternative. CamelCase notation begins with a description (with the first letter in the "lower case," when it's a local, private variable—hence the name "CamelCase") and usually ends with the object type *unabbreviated*. For example, the variable in Listing 2-5 refers to chart on a worksheet for sales.

Listing 2-5. A Demonstration of Camel Back Notation

```
Dim salesChart as Excel.Chart
Set salesChart = Sheet1.ChartObjects(1).Chart
```

I'll be honest and admit I'm not always such a stickler about that lower case descriptor, which is why I call my use of this notation "loose." The important takeaway when using this notation is to use *very descriptive names*. It's unlikely a variable name like ChartTitle will be confused for an integer in your code. Whether it's recordCount or RecordCount, you'll likely understand that count refers to a nonnegative integer.

My rule of thumb is, local primitive types should start with a lower case, if you feel so inclined. Variables that represent objects should end with the object name *unabbreviated*. Notice in Listing 2-5 that the variable name ends with Chart. Ranges should end with Range, etc.

Descriptive names are important. Use a variable name that describes what the variable does so when you come back to it later, you can remember what you did. If you have a test variable, then (please, for the love of God) call it "test,"; don't just call it "t." It's OK to use i in a For/Next loop where the i is simply an iterator and is not used later in the code, but don't name variables used to count objects with short names like i,j,k,a,b,c. Finally, there's really no good reason to use an underscore in your variable names. They're not easier to read.

Named Ranges

As I said above, naming convention goes beyond just VBA. Indeed, a proper naming convention should be applied to all Excel objects, including those that reside on a spreadsheet. Therefore, in this section, I'll talk about naming objects on the spreadsheet in the form of named ranges.

It's rather common to see Excel developers use the prefix "val" to refer to named cell ranges. This prefix is an attempt to extend the Hungarian Notation principles into the physical spreadsheet (as if we haven't already had enough of it!). However, I still prefer a more modern approach. Specifically, what I like to do is combine the name of the tab and the function of the variable in to be object-oriented-like. Figure 2-10 shows a good example of what I mean.

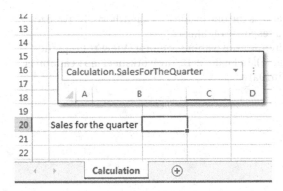

Figure 2-10. *An object-oriented like naming convetion for named ranges*

In Figure 2-10, the name of the tab is combined with the variable. Aside from being more object-oriented-ish, this type of naming brings other distinct advantages. For one, you can more easily and logically group named ranges that exist on the same worksheet tab. In addition, as you'll see in the next section, this type of convention works very well when interfacing between named ranges and VBA.

Sheet Objects

In this section, I'll focus on naming conventions for sheet objects. There's one property of the sheet object that I'm a big fan of changing, and it's the name of the object itself. When you change the name of a worksheet tab on the spreadsheet, you're actually changing the name of the tab (think of it as changing a caption); you are not, in fact, changing the name of the worksheet object itself.

If for nothing else, changing the name of the worksheet object is a great way to clear up confusion when looking at the Project Explorer window. For example, Excel seems to have a problem keeping the names of worksheet tabs and the names of the objects themselves straight, as I'm sure you've noticed before. Take a look at Figure 2-11 to see what I mean.

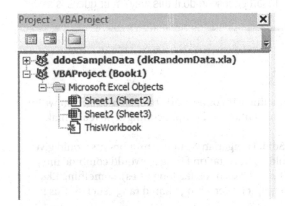

Figure 2-11. *The Project Explorer demonstrating a lack of consistency when it comes to worksheet object and tab names*

The *object* name is the item outside the parenthesis; the tab name is the one inside the parenthesis. If I were to write `MsgBox Sheet1.Name` in the Immediate window, I would see a response of "Sheet2."

To change the name of the object itself, go to the Properties window from within the editor (View ➤ Properties Window, if it's not already visible) and change the line that says (name). In Figure 2-12, my worksheet tab's caption is "Financial Data," so I'm going to change its object name to `FinancialData`.

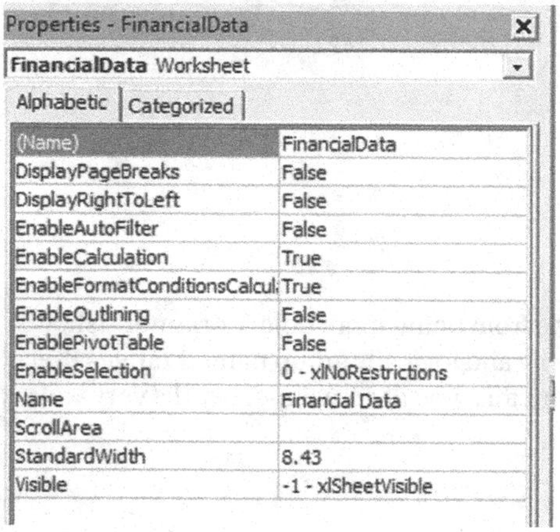

Figure 2-12. *The Properties Explorer showing how to change the worksheet object's name*

YES, I KNOW IT'S CONFUSING

If you look at the Project Explorer window (Figure 2-12, above), you'll see that the worksheet object name comes first and the tab name follows in parenthesis. The Properties Explorer window appears to do just the opposite; the first name in parenthesis, "(name)", refers to the object's name, while the second name item (under Enable Selection) refers to its name as it appears on the tab. Why did Microsoft choose to do it this way? Your guess is as good as mine.

Referencing

In this section, I'll talk about referencing. Referencing refers to interacting with other worksheet elements from within VBA code and also on the worksheet. This is where a good naming convention and proper coding style really makes the difference.

Let's take a made-up named range concerning Cost of Goods Sold. Hungarian Notation proponents would give the named range something like `valCoGS` (CoGS = Cost of Goods Sold). The notation I suggest would combine the tab name with a nicely descriptive title (you could make it shorter if you'd like, but I like long titles), something like `IncomeStatement.CostOfGoodsSold`. So let's take a look at why you might prefer a long named range such as this in the next section.

Shorthand References

This section discusses shorthand references, a syntax you can use in your code to refer named range on a sheet. Here is where the advantage of the latter notation proves its worth. As you know, you can refer to a named range through the sheet object where the name resides (technically, you can refer to it through any sheet object, but only on the worksheet in which it was created will it return the correct information). So, the typical way to read from or assign to the Cost of Goods Sold named range above using Hungarian Notation might look like this this:

```
Worksheets("Income Statement").Range("valCoGS").Value
```

On the other hand, if you use my method, you can employ the shorthand range syntax as follows:

```
[IncomeStatement.CostOfGoodsSold].Value
```

That's right! These two lines of code mean and do the exact same thing. Now, which do you think is easier to read and is more descriptive of what it represents? Which more easily captures the worksheet in which it resides? Which would you rather use in your code?

Ok, so before you go off using the shorthand notation for everything, I should point out a significant caveat. Using the shorthand brackets method can become, in certain situations, slow. Technically, it's a slower operation for Excel to complete than using a Worksheet object. However, you would really only notice this if you use the shorthand notation during a very long and computationally expensive loop. For typical code looping, you're not likely to see the difference, but if you're looking to speed things up inside a loop, it's best to forgo the shorthand.

Worksheet Object Names

In the previous section, I showed you how to change the worksheet object names. In this section, you'll see why I think it's such a good idea.

Think about what you can do with this change. Because the new name reflects some descriptive information about the worksheet tab, you can use the object itself instead of the Worksheets() function to return the one you're interested in. Confused? Let's take a look. Here's the old way, which takes in the Worksheet's tab name to return the worksheet object:

```
Worksheets("Income Statement").Range("A1")
```

And here's what you can do instead:

```
IncomeStatement.Range("A1")
```

Again, which do you think easier to understand and work with?

Procedures and Macros

In this section, I'll talk about the benefit of changing sheet names on procedures. Once you've changed the procedure name, you can also place your macro into the sheet object itself.

Take a look at how cleanly these procedures appear in the Macro dialog box versus the ones housed in a sheet object with a default name in Figure 2-13. In addition, if you want to call a public procedure stored in a sheet object, you can simply write IncomeStatement.CalculateNetTotal from within the code of another sheet object (or module) in Excel. I'll talk about the benefits of storing a procedure in a sheet object (versus a module) in the next section.

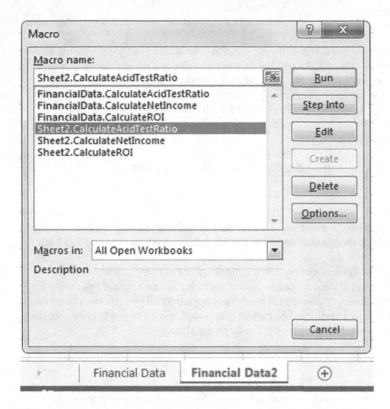

Figure 2-13. *A demonstration of changing worksheet tab names and storing procedures therein*

Development Styles and Principles

Now that you've set up your coding environment and I've talked about naming conventions, I need to talk development styles and principles. The following is a list of simple coding guidelines that if you stick to, you'll be creating self-contained, easy-to-follow code and design in no time. The first principle follows naturally from the last section.

Strive to Store Your Commonly Used Procedures in Relevant Worksheet Tabs

If you're an avid user of the Macro Recorder you know that Excel writes what you do to an open module. In many ways, a module feels like a natural place for a procedure. But ask yourself, is there any real reason why you're storing the procedure there?

The problem with storing your procedures in a module is that it creates really sloppy code. I know what you're thinking: how dare I say that! You separate your modules into different logical pieces. The items inside each of your well-named modules are relevant to one another. Chances are, though, the procedures in your model are only used by one or two spreadsheets. If that's the case, why not store the procedures in the worksheet objects themselves?

Consider this example I've seen time and time again. You have a Main worksheet tab that acts as a menu to direct users to several other worksheet tabs. Then, in each of these tabs, you have a button that takes users back to the Main worksheet. Let's use the tabs from Figure 2-14 for this example.

Figure 2-14. *A common spreadsheet layout in which Main acts a menu to take users to each tab*

If you create this direction mechanism via the module method, you get ugly navigational code like in Listing 2-6. I also assume in Listing 2-6 that you're doing some type of processing work where the user goes from a different worksheet tab back to Main.

Listing 2-6. Ugly Navigational Code

```
' Links from Main screen
Public Sub From_Main_Goto_Config()
    Worksheets("Config").Activate
End Sub
Public Sub From_Main_Goto_Edit()
    Worksheets("Edit").Activate
End Sub
Public Sub From_Main_Goto_View()
    Worksheets("View").Activate
End Sub
Public Sub From_Main_Goto_Options()
    Worksheets("Options").Activate
End Sub

'Link back to Main from each screen
Public Sub From_Config_Goto_Main()
    .
    .
    .
    Worksheets("Main").Activate
End Sub
Public Sub From_Edit_Goto_Main()
    .
    .
    .
    Worksheets("Main").Activate
End Sub
Public Sub From_View_Goto_Main()
    .
    .
    .
    Worksheets("Main").Activate
End Sub
Public Sub From_Option_Goto_Main()
    .
    .
    .
    Worksheets("Main").Activate
End Sub
```

What do I mean by ugly? Well, creating this mechanism in a module requires you use funky procedure names to differentiate one from the other. And just take a look at what each of these procedures look like in the Macro dialog box (Figure 2-15). Each of these names looks so similar. It would be very easy to accidentally assign the wrong macro. (Are you nodding your head because you've done it before!? I know your pain.) In addition, even if you store procedures in separate modules, there's nothing in the Macro dialog box to differentiate for this type of organization.

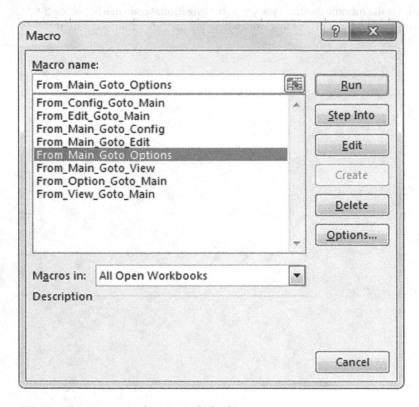

Figure 2-15. *A mess in the Macro dialog box*

But now, let's take a look at my suggested improvements (including changing the worksheet names above). You can store the procedures that take you from the Main tab to other worksheet tabs in the Main worksheet object (Figure 2-16).

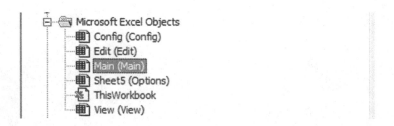

Figure 2-16. *A view from Project Explorer when the worksheet object names are changed*

As well, you can use much cleaner-looking procedure headings, as shown in Listing 2-7.

Listing 2-7. Cleaner Code Now Stored in the Main Worksheet Object

```
Public Sub SendToConfig()
    Config.Activate
End Sub
Public Sub SendToEdit()
    Edit.Activate
End Sub
Public Sub SendToView()
    View.Activate
End Sub
Public Sub SendToOptions()
    Options.Activate
End Sub
```

Next, in each separate worksheet object you would simply use something like the following procedure in Listing 2-8. As a matter of proper style, you should use the same name, BackToMain, in each worksheet object. Remember, unlike in modules, procedure names in worksheet objects aren't global. Because of this, you can use the same name across different worksheets.

Listing 2-8. BackToMain Stored in Each Separate Procedure. Takes the User Back to the Main Page

```
Public Sub BackToMain()
.
.
.
    Main.Activate
End Sub.
```

Take a look at Figure 2 8. As you can see, each procedure is much easier to read and understand right away from within the Macro dialog box. In addition, notice how you've made the code more object-oriented-like. Each tab that you can navigate to from Main shares the same procedure. It's as if they are of a similar class. When you add extra procedures to the worksheet (but keep the one sending users back home) you are *inheriting* the features of each sheet and then adding new ones to it.

Figure 2-17. The Macro dialog box showing a much clearn presentation and organization of code and procedure names

And another thing...

You thought I was done complaining about putting procedures in modules, didn't you? Well, I'm not. Because there's another problem we need to address head on in this section. So let's do that by taking a quick survey. Grab a pen to mark down your answers. If this is a library book, upon returning the book, tell them you found it this way.

THE ACTIVE OBJECT STRESS TEST

Circle all that apply.

I ran a macro that uses the Selection object. However, I (or the user) selected the <u>wrong</u> worksheet item (either manually or in the code) and accidentally made undoable changes to everything. This makes me feel

a. Annoyed

b. REPT("I want to scream!", 1000)

c. Like I never want to use the Selection object again!

I ran a macro that uses the ActiveSheet object, but accidentally I was looking at the wrong sheet before running the macro. Also, I forgot to save everything before running the macro, so now I have start over. I feel

a. Exhausted

b. REPT("I want to scream!", 1000)

c. Totally done using ActiveSheet, forever!

I ran a macro that uses ActiveCell, but the wrong cell was selected for some unforgivable reason. The code made changes to that cell and a whole bunch of cells around it. Unwittingly, I ended up making incorrect and undoable changes to the entire spreadsheet. I feel

a. Terrible

b. REPT("I want to scream!", 1000)

c. I'm so over using ActiveCell.

Now take a look at your answers. If you circled C for any of the above questions, you're in luck. I have some really great news for you in the next section.

No More Using the ActiveSheet, ActiveCell, ActiveWorkbook, and Selection Objects

You don't need these objects; in this section, you'll see why. It's often the case that coding inside a module encourages you to use these objects, since the procedures themselves aren't worksheet-specific. But if you're already working inside the procedure (as I suggest above) you can use the Me object. Me is always the container object in which your code is housed. For example, if the following code were in Sheet1, the Me object refers to Sheet1.

```
Me.Range("A1").Value = "Hello Me!"
```

That's not all, either. You can use ThisWorkbook instead of ActiveWorkbook to ensure you are always modifying the workbook in which your code resides. If you want to modify a cell, address it directly like I've done in the code above. If you want to refer to a chart or shape, why select it first? Which gets to the point more easily, Listing 2-9 or Listing 2-10?

Listing 2-9. Using Selection and Active Objects

```
ActiveWorkbook.Worksheets("Sheet1").Activate
ActiveSheet.Shapes("Shape1").Select
Selection.Fill.ForeColor.RGB = RGB(0, 0, 0)
```

Listing 2-10. Referencing Objects Directly

```
Me.Shapes("Shape1").Fill.ForeColor.RGB = RGB(0, 0, 0)
...
Dim salesChart As Excel.Chart
Set salesChart = [SalesChart].Chart
```

Isn't VBA great? It sure is, but not for everything. That brings me to the next principle.

Render Unto Excel the Things that are Excel's, and Unto VBA the Things that Require VBA

VBA lets you do a lot, but it's not a great idea to do everything in VBA, especially when it involves reinventing the wheel. For instance, it's tempting to store your all your program's global variables in a module. This method brings the advantage of total and complete accessibility: the variables can be accessed anywhere at any time by any procedure.

However, these variables are also "freed" from memory whenever your code errors out or whenever you tell Excel to "reset (Figure 2-18). When this memory is dumped, you must start over—those variables once again become zeros or blanks. Often those who use this method must create an Initialize or Restore procedure to restore the correct values to these variables before one can do anything else in the spreadsheet.

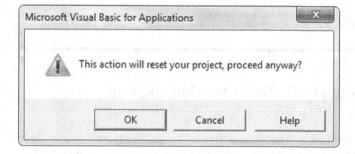

Figure 2-18. *Hitting OK will reset the values of all those public variables stored in procedures*

There's a better way, people. I don't need to tell you that Excel is a giant storage closet. It's a much better idea to store your application models *on the spreadsheet* instead of in the module where they are susceptible to being cleared out every time there's an error. Just create a new tab to hold your backend variables. Name it something like Calculations, Variables, Constants—you get the picture. Then use the shorthand range syntax discussed above to access these ranges. It couldn't be simpler. And it brings an additional benefit worth mentioning in my next principle.

Encapsulating Your Work

Encapsulation is a tenant of object-oriented programming that argues (1) associated data and procedures should be organized together, and (2) access to and manipulation of the former items should be restricted or granted in only certain circumstances. By coupling together relevant procedures into a relevant worksheet tab, you fulfill the first item.

The second item is fulfilled when you store application variables on the worksheet. This is because the only way to change these variables is by either writing to them with code or updating them manually behind the scenes. Let's say you have a named ranged called `Calculate.Input`. I can change this variable's value in the code (see below), which requires I run a macro.

```
[Calculate.Input] = 1
```

Or I can change its value by finding it on the spreadsheet and typing in something new, as in Figure 2-19.

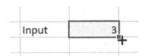

Figure 2-19. *A worskheet named range variable called Calc.Input*

However, if I want to access this variable somewhere else on the worksheet, I must access it through a formula, like this:

```
= Calc.Input - 1
```

Notice that this simply accesses the value stored in `Calc.Input`—it doesn't change the value itself. However, it's impossible with a formula to change the value of `Calc.Input`. Like I said above, there are only two ways to change its value, a macro or a human. This is an example of encapsulation.

The Last Word

In this chapter, I talked about how to set up your coding experience to make the most of it, proper naming conventions, and development styles and principles. Some of these suggestions were counterintuitive to what is commonly taught, but explanations on why they were useful for what we do were given. I don't expect you to leave this chapter entirely convinced, but hopefully you see the value in developing good coding practices—and why sometimes doing things differently makes sense.

CHAPTER 3

■ ■ ■

Introducing Formula Concepts

Q: What does every newborn spreadsheet need?

A: Formula

Spreadsheet formulas hold a unique place in advanced Excel development. Most of us are familiar with formulas as a means to produce results more quickly than with manual calculation. For example, if we want to find the arithmetic sum of a range, does it make sense to pull out the Burroughs Adding Machine and punch in each item one by one? No. The very nature of a spreadsheet provides a built-in means to manipulate its elements.

Most of us are used to this type of manipulation with formulas; that is, we use formulas as a means to find and return results. Spreadsheet formulas, when used for Excel development, however, do much more. They form the infrastructure upon which much of our work is based.

Throughout this book we will be working with formulas. Some of these formulas will be very complex. When you first start, they may appear daunting. However, practice makes perfect, and experience is your greatest teacher. The more you use them, the more you develop a formula literacy. What may have appeared hard to read at first glance should become easier. But more important than knowing the formulas themselves is understanding the concepts behind what drives them.

And, of course, Excel includes a few tools and features to help you understand your formulas. Let's go through a few of them you can start using now.

Formula Help

In this section, I'll talk about making the most of your formula experience. The following tips should make your life easier, especially when working with complex formulas.

F2 to See the Formula of a Select Cell

Chances are you're already pretty familiar with F2. But for the uninitiated, pressing the F2 key on a cell containing a formula will highlight the portions of a spreadsheet upon which the formula depends. If you're trying to evaluate a formula, F2 is a good first start to your investigation.

F9 for On-Demand and Piecewise Calculation

F9 is the shortcut key to tell Excel to recalculate. If you type =RANDBETWEEN(1,2) in an empty cell on an Excel worksheet and then press F9 continuously, you will see that cell update to 1 or 2 at random. (In addition, if you have any other volatile formulas, those will update too).

F9 can also provide a piecewise, or partial, calculation of a long formula. Take the seemingly complex formula shown in Listing 3-1.

Listing 3-1. An Example of a Long, Complex Formula

```
=IF(SUMPRODUCT(A1:A3*(B1:B3>2))>7, CONCATENATE(A2 & L3), IFERROR(C6, "An error occurred."))
```

Let's say you want to evaluate only a part of this formula, specifically the highlighted portion of the same formula but now in Excel's formula bar (Figure 3-1).

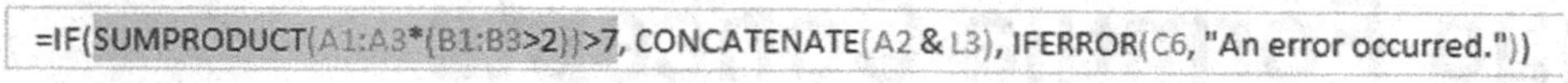

=IF(SUMPRODUCT(A1:A3*(B1:B3>2))>7, CONCATENATE(A2 & L3), IFERROR(C6, "An error occurred."))

Figure 3-1. *You can select a portion of the formula to be evaluated immediately*

In fact, you can tell Excel to evaluate just that easily. If you highlight the portion as I've done in Figure 3-1, you can press F9 to see what it evaluates to (see Figure 3-2).

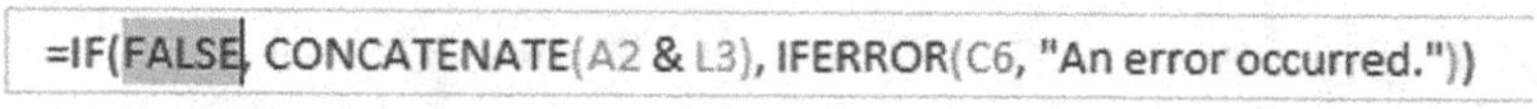

=IF(FALSE, CONCATENATE(A2 & L3), IFERROR(C6, "An error occurred."))

Figure 3-2. *Pressing F9 on the highlighted portion evaluates the highlighted portion immediately*

You now see this portion evaluates to False. In the formula bar, Excel just rewrites this portion of highlighted text to read "FALSE." And you can do this to any portion of the formula. If you click outside the formula bar or press the escape key, the formula will return to its original, unevaluated text. F9 then, when used with formulas, is the ultimate on-demand approach for quick formula evaluation.

Evaluate Formula Button

The Evaluate Formula button allows you to step through an entire formula. Here's how it works. First, click the cell you're interested in investigating. Then, click the Formulas tab on the ribbon. Go to Evaluate Formulas in the Formula Auditing group. Take a look at Figure 3-3.

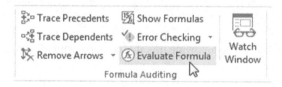

Figure 3-3. *The Evaluate Formula button*

A dialog box similar to the one shown in Figure 3-4 should appear. The underlined portion is the current expression to be evaluated. If available, you can go deeper into the formula by pressing the Step In button. You can Step Out if that level of granularity is no longer need. For formulas that resolve to an error, the Evaluate Formula tool can be very helpful to understand the conditions right before the error. I find Evaluate Formula an indispensable part of my Excel Development toolkit.

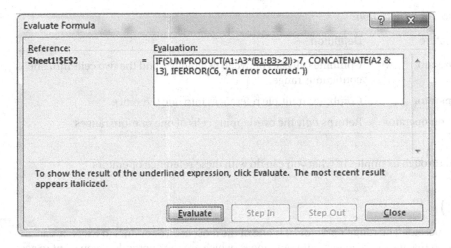

Figure 3-4. *The Evaluate Formula dialog box*

Excel Formula Concepts

In this section, I'll talk about formula concepts you'll be using throughout the rest of this book. To begin, Excel formulas are made up of four main types:

- Functions, such as AVERAGE( ), SUM( ), IF( )

- Constants and literals, such as number, string, and Boolean values like 2, 100, 1E7, "Hello world", and FALSE

- References, such as A1 or A1:A20

- Operators, such as +, -, /, >, :

You're probably already familiar with several of these types. Obviously, functions make up a huge part of formula use. Constants that are numbers are also probably familiar. However, did you know that Boolean values like TRUE and FALSE are also constants? Finally, you've probably used references and operations many times by now, but did you know the colon (:) that forms the range A1:A20 is also an operator?

Operators, in Depth

This section will discuss Excel operators. You're probably familiar with Excel's arithmetic operators, plus (+), minus (-), times (*), and divide (/). But besides arithmetic operators, Excel has a *text* and three *reference* operators.

Excel's text operator is the ampersand (&), which stands in for the CONCATENATE function. For instance, the formulas =A1&B1 and =CONCATENATE(A1,B1) do the exact same thing. You've probably also used Excel's reference operators many times, the colon (:) in particular, without thinking of them as operators. Excel's two other reference operators are the comma (,) and space ( ) characters. Table 3-1 talks about what they do.

Table 3-1. *Reference Operators and Their Descritions*

Reference Operator	Nomenclature	Definition
: (colon)	Range operator	Combines all cells between two ranges, and the two cells into one contiguous range.
, (comma)	Union operator	Combines multiple references into one reference.
(space)	Intersection operator	Returns *only* the overlapping cells of one or more ranges.

In the next few sections, I'll go through examples of what you can do with these reference operators.

The Range Operator (:)

In this section, I discuss the range operator. The range operator (:) is one of the most used operators in Excel. It's an operator in every sense of the word in that it acts upon two different ranges (which are the operands, if you want to get technical) and returns a contiguous range. What's so great about the range operator is that you can actually combine functions, like

```
= A1:INDEX(A:A, COUNTA(A:A))
```

and

```
= B1:OFFSET(B:B, COUNTA(B:B), 0)
```

So let's take a look at an example that shows the power of the range operator.

EXAMPLE: DYNAMICALLY SIZED RANGES

Using the range operator, you can create dynamically sized ranges. This means you can create a range that can grow and shrink as the list they represent is added to or subtracted from. Both the INDEX and OFFSET formulas can help you with this mechanism. In this example, they both work about the same way.

Consider the range in Figure 3-5.

◢	A	B	C
1	My Favorite Colors		
2	Red		
3	Orange		
4	Yellow		
5	Green		
6	Blue		
7	Indigo		
8	Violate		
9			
10			

Figure 3-5. *A sample set of data upon which you will create a dynamically sized range*

If I want a count of all my favorite colors in this example (in real life, I have only one favorite color, and *it's black*), I can use the COUNTA function on the range A2 to A8. But what if I want to add to the list? In that case, I must reapply my formula to accommodate the next color in cell A9. Alternatively, I can just say something like A2:A1000, where the second range is an arbitrarily large number. Neither the former's formula reapplication nor the latter's arbitrarily high number are very good fixes.

The best solution is to use a dynamically sized range. To do this with the INDEX formula, you can write =$A$2:INDEX($A:$A,COUNTA($A:$A)) like in Figure 3-6.

▲	A	B	C	D	E	F
1	My Favorite Colors					
2	Red		=$A$2:INDEX($A:$A,COUNTA($A:$A))			
3	Orange					
4	Yellow					
5	Green					
6	Blue					
7	Indigo					
8	Violate					

Figure 3-6. A demonstration of the formula that will ultimately help you create a dynamically sized range

Here's how it works. You supply the entire column range A:A to the INDEX formula. In the row argument of the INDEX formula, you're interested in the last row of content in the column range of A:A. COUNTA, which counts every filled cell in the range supplied to it, will return an 8, since the last row of content is the eighth row down. When you use INDEX, you're probably used to its returning values. If you hadn't added that A1 at the beginning of the formula, the INDEX function by itself would have simply returned the word "Violate." But behind the scenes, Excel is actually returning a *reference* to the cell containing "Violate," not just its value. So, effectively, Excel is returns A8, which becomes A1:A8 in the formula.

When you press Enter, you'll probably see the formula return the value Red. This is because it's returning the top of the range. If you continue to drag the formula down, you'll see that it returns the other cells in the range too (if it doesn't, select the entire range and press Ctrl+Shift+Enter). But to really use dynamically sized ranges to your advantage, you can assign them to a named range as I've done in Figure 3-7. Make sure when you do it the cell references are absolute.

Edit Name		?	X
Name:	myNamedRange		
Scope:	Workbook ▾		
Comment:			
Refers to:	=Sheet1!$A$2:INDEX(Sheet1!$A:$A,COUNTA(Sheet1!$A:$A))		
	OK	Cancel	

Figure 3-7. Creating a new named range out of the formula

You can then use that named range elsewhere on your spreadsheet. For example, in cell C8 in Figure 3-8, I've used the formula =COUNTA(myNamedRange). As you can see, I've added to my list, and the count has updated automatically. Just imagine using these dynamically sized ranges in charts, dropdowns, and formulas! You'll get to do that in the next chapter.

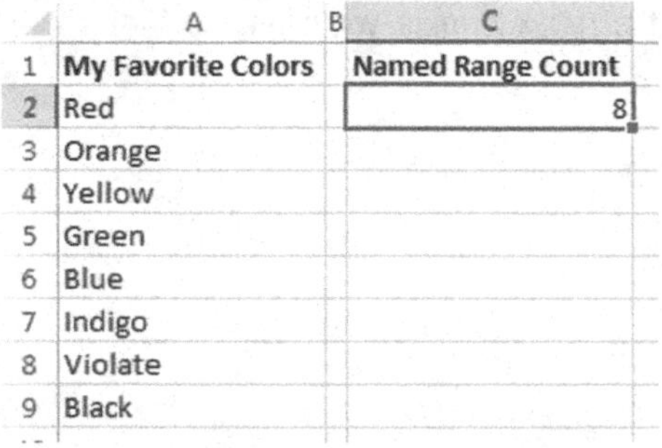

	A	B	C
1	My Favorite Colors		Named Range Count
2	Red		8
3	Orange		
4	Yellow		
5	Green		
6	Blue		
7	Indigo		
8	Violate		
9	Black		

Figure 3-8. *Using the Name Range elsewhere*

You can do the same with OFFSET, using this formula:

```
=$A$2:OFFSET($A$1,COUNTA($A:$A),0)
```

Experiment a little and see if you can figure this one out. Remember, if you need help, use the formula help suggestions from the beginning of the chapter.

A final note is in order. There's also some argument on whether INDEX is faster than OFFSET, since OFFSET is a volatile function (that means it will recalculate every time the sheet recalculates) and INDEX is not. In general, I prefer INDEX for this reason.

The Union Operator (,)

The union operator (,) is also likely familiar to you. The formula =SUM(A1:A10,C1:C5) employs the union operator to combine the two disparate ranges into one range upon which to take the sum. Unlike the range operator, which forms a contiguous range between two cells, the union operator essentially turns the two noncontiguous ranges into one long range. Think of it like this:

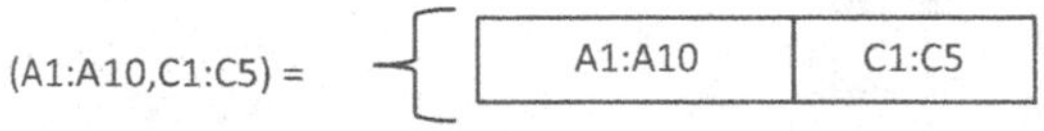

(A1:A10,C1:C5) =

A1:A10	C1:C5

In this next section, I'll talk about how you can use the union operation to your advantage.

EXAMPLE: PULLING RANK

Let's say you wanted to find where a certain number ranks within a series of numbers, when they're ordered. For example, if you have an unsorted series of numbers (8,4,6,1, and 2), you can use Excel's RANK function to find where the number 6 resides in a descending list of these numbers.

In Figure 3-9, I have the formula =RANK(D2,$A$2:$A$6) in cell D2.

	A	B	C	D
1	Number Series			
2	8		Input Num	6
3	4		Rank	2
4	6			
5	1			
6	2			

Figure 3-9. A demonstration of finding the rank of a given number within an unsorted list

RANK will automatically turn the range in the given series in descending order (by default, descending is selected; however, this can be changed in RANK's third, optional parameter). The rank of the number 6 then is 2, as shown in Figure 3-10.

8 **6** 4 1 2

Six is highlighted and is in the second place in the region.

Figure 3-10. A visual representation of how this example works

This function only works when the input number (in D2 above) is a number in the set of the five given numbers. But what if you want to find where the number 4.4 resides in the ordered series? The formula, left as is, will return an NA() error if D2 is set to 4.4. To get around this, you need to add the input number to the set of numbers. You can do this with the union operator, like so:

=RANK(D2,($A$2:$A$6,D2))

If D2 = 4.4, the series ($A$2:$A$6,D2) becomes 8, 6, **4.4**, 4, 1, 2, which returns the number 3. Consider how this formula might be useful. If you have a list times, dates, or temperatures and want to return certain information when an input value is between two boundaries, you can do that with this formula.

The Intersection Operator ( )

The intersection operator ( ), demonstrated as one space, returns one or more cells from overlapping ranges. Figure 3-11 shows that the intersection of range D2:D6 and B4:F4 is 3. You can verify that both of the ranges intersect, or overlap, at cell D4.

H4
=D2:D6 B4:F4
A B C D E F G H I J
1
2 1
3 2
4 4 5 3 6 7 3
5 4
6 5

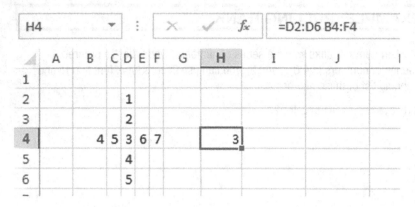

***Figure 3-11.** The intersection operator in action*

You'll learn a creative use for the intersection operator in this next example.

INTERSECTING REGIONS AND MONTHS

Let's say you have a table of units sold by month and region, like in Figure 3-12.

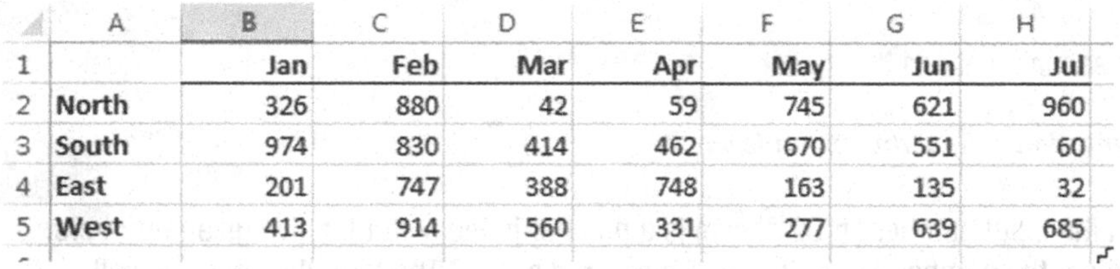

A B C D E F G H
1 Jan Feb Mar Apr May Jun Jul
2 North 326 880 42 59 745 621 960
3 South 974 830 414 462 670 551 60
4 East 201 747 388 748 163 135 32
5 West 413 914 560 331 277 639 685

***Figure 3-12.** A sample set of regional and monthly data*

To save time, you've had a macro assign columns B through H to be the named ranges Jan, Feb, Mar... etc. You've done the same thing for each region, assigning the row ranges to North, South, East, and West.

Then, if you're interested in the sum total of units sold in the East region on January and March, you can use the formula `=SUM(East Jan:March)`, as shown in Figure 3-13.

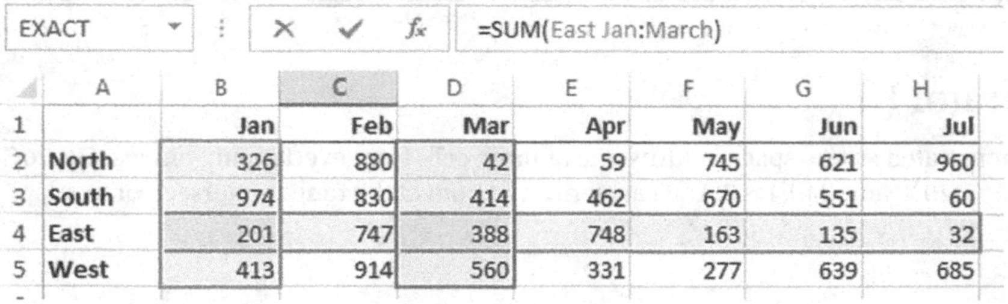

EXACT
=SUM(East Jan:March)
A B C D E F G H
1 Jan Feb Mar Apr May Jun Jul
2 North 326 880 42 59 745 621 960
3 South 974 830 414 462 670 551 60
4 East 201 747 388 748 163 135 32
5 West 413 914 560 331 277 639 685

***Figure 3-13.** An application of the union operator on sample regional and monthly data*

The formula returns 1366, which is the sum of 201, 747, and 388. If you want to see the performance for the eastern region for just the months of January and March but not February, you can use the following formula:

```
=SUM(East Jan + East March)
```

If you're particularly mathematically minded, and hopefully you will be somewhat by the end of the next chapter, you can simplify this formula like so:

```
=SUM(East (Jan, March))
```

Note that `East Jan + East March = East (Jan, March)`, which parallels the Distributive Law of algebra. I'll go into this in a little more detail later in the next chapter.

When to Use Conditional Expressions

In this section, you're going to dive deeper into conditional expressions. If you've used IF, then you've used a conditional expression before. Conditional expressions are all about testing things. For example, in the formula =IF(AB>2, "Yes", "No"), the first argument, AB>2, is the conditional expression. Any expression that uses the logic operators, =, <, >, etc., is a conditional expression.

So you want to test the value of a cell and return a result if it passes a test or another result if it fails. Quick: *which function should you use?*

Was your answer IF? *If* it was, then you're not alone. The IF function feels like a natural choice, especially because the first parameter of the IF function calls for a logical expression. But there are also some instances where IF isn't the best choice. The Excel MVP, Daniel Ferry, has gone so far as to argue that the IF function is the most overused function of all. And, as this chapter will demonstrate, there's good reason to believe this.

Deceptively Simple Nested IF Statements

One supposed advantage to using the IF function is the ability to make use of nesting conditions. For example, if I have multiple compounding conditions, I can place IF statements inside the value_if_true and value_if_false parameters (Listing 3-2). In my experience, however, IF statements are nested far more often than they need to be.

Listing 3-2. A Prototype of the IF Function

```
IF(logical_test, value_if_true, value_if_false)
```

Even I have to admit that nested IF statements are unavoidable. But I like to save them for formulas that exhibit natural branching conditions. Consider

```
=IF(ProjectStatus = "Stopped", IF(Err_Code=1, "Halted by internal error.","Uknown error."),
"Project has NOT finished.")
```

I would argue this is a good example of the problem with using nested IF statements. Its inherent logic naturally represents a branching condition (see Figure 3-14).

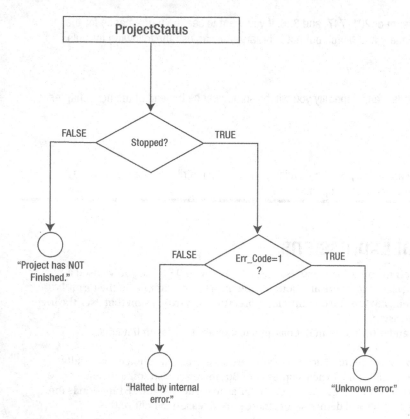

Figure 3-14. A flowchart showing the branching conditions of your IF statement

Sometimes it's not always so clear whether the problems represent a compound branching condition. A good rule of thumb is to start from one of the possible results and work backwards. Ask yourself: does the result naturally follow from the test condition? In other words: does this result make sense given the conditions?

Confused? I hear you. Well, let's consider the following example from Microsoft's very own help guide, shown in Listing 3-3.

Listing 3-3. An Example of Nested IFs from Microsoft's Excel Help

```
=IF(A2>89,"A",IF(A2>79,"B", IF(A2>69,"C",IF(A2>59,"D","F"))))
```

This formula returns a letter grade based on a student's raw grade stored in A2. It's a good example of a problem that makes for a poor branching condition. The grade you receive isn't the result of *not receiving another grade*. (I know you're scratching your head here but bear with me for a moment). Your letter grade is the result of where your score falls within one of five different numerical boundaries. If anything, this is a lookup problem. You could easily employ the RANK function example from above or use the MATCH function. But if you were to frame this problem organically, the reason a student receives an F is not because they didn't receive a D, C, B, or A. The IF function above turns this lookup problem into a branching condition problem when it needn't be.

Another common example involves using states as numbers. Consider the formula in Listing 3-4.

Listing 3-4. Another Example Using IFs That Isn't a Branching Condition

```
=IF(A2=1, "Small",IF(A2=2,"Med", "Large")).
```

In this example, A2 holds an encoded Id or state. For an example like this, the states could be anything, but they usually form some natural *ordinal* scale. In the example above, the Ids map to the following results: 1=**Small**, 2=**Medium**, and 3=**Large**. We call these categories ordinal because they can be ordered naturally. Here again, IF is not a good choice. The problem presented is not a branching condition but rather a test of scale. Indeed, for formulas like these, the CHOOSE function is a much better choice.

CHOOSE Wisely

In this section, I'll go through how to use CHOOSE, and why for some situations it makes for a better choice than IF. CHOOSE is much like IF, but it can more naturally deal with ordinal data. Listing 3-5 includes the prototype for CHOOSE.

Listing 3-5. CHOOSE( ) Prototype

```
CHOOSE(index_num, value1, value2,...)
```

CHOOSE analyzes the argument supplied to the index_num parameter and returns the value at the given index number. In the example above, when index_num is 1, value1 is returned; when index_num is 2, value2 is returned, and so forth.

In the previous instance, you could simply write =CHOOSE(A2, "Small", "Med", "Large"). This appears to be more closely align with the way this example is naturally formulated. Because of this, CHOOSE makes the data arrangement more easy to read and understand at first glance. Compare the two arrangements:

IF arrangement

```
=IF(A2=1, "Small",IF(A2=2,"Med", "Large")).
```

CHOOSE arrangement

```
=CHOOSE(A2, "Small", "Med", "Large")
```

GENERATING RANDOM DATA WITH CHOOSE()

CHOOSE is also great for generating random categorical or nominal data. This type of random data generation is particularly useful to create test data for your dashboard backend database. All it takes is the addition of the RANDBETWEEN function. Say you have categorical data of Big, Medium, and Little. You could generate data with the following formula:

```
=CHOOSE(RANDBETWEEN(1,3), "Big", "Medium", "Little")
```

Why This Discussion Is Important

Like the IF statement, CHOOSE can be useful for elements that appear on your next spreadsheet dashboard, decision support tool, or application.

A nested IF condition will attempt to evaluate every condition until a true value results or terminates to the end of the nest. CHOOSE makes one evaluation and goes to the specified index. On its face, CHOOSE would seem superior for scenarios in which a nested condition isn't necessary. Fewer evaluations means fewer instructions for Excel to complete. In previous versions of Excel and on older machines, conserving machine processing by using optimal formula structures really did seem to make a difference. However, now that we've entered the age of multithreaded processers, I must admit the performance differences have become less noticeable.

So then why have I made the distinction? Well, using the formula that best matches what you're trying to accomplish **just makes sense**. In addition, and perhaps more importantly, when you come back to your formula later after having been away from your spreadsheet for a while, a formula that better matches your test conditions will ultimately be easier to once again comprehend, especially if it's complex in nature.

Ok, you're not convinced. I wasn't at first, either. In the end, there may not be a noticeable difference between using IF or CHOOSE, I admit. But in the previous chapter I turned conventional coding on its head. And I'll keep doing so throughout this book.

And if you're tempted to keep using IF, read on. Chances are you'll find it at least one example in which IF isn't necessary.

Introduction to Boolean Concepts

In this section, I'll talk about concepts surrounding Boolean expressions. For the unfamiliar, Boolean formulas use a type of mathematical logic called Boolean algebra and they're the natural result of *conditional expressions*.

The most important feature of a Boolean expression is that it always returns one of two mutually exclusive values: either it returns TRUE, or it returns FALSE. Excel, however, brings another important twist to the TRUE/FALSE dynamic. *Sometimes* TRUE can also mean the number one, and FALSE can also mean the number zero. Let's take a look in the following example.

FILTERING ODD OR EVEN VALUES

Booleans are great for filtering. Take a look at Figure 3-15. In this example, I've created a mechanism to only show either odd or even values in the accompanying chart.

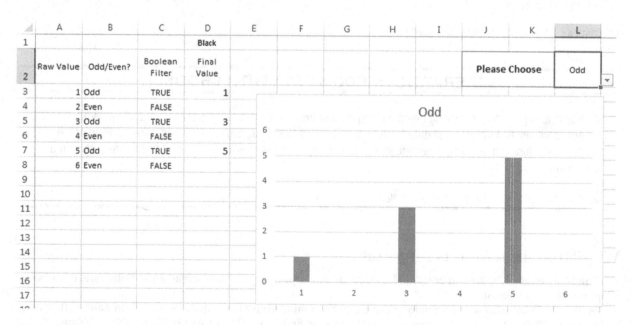

Figure 3-15. *Booleans used for filtering*

I provide the user a dropdown box to select between either showing odd values or even values. On the left, I've included a table that helps evaluate what the final chart will show. Figure 3-16 shows this table in more detail.

	A	B	C	D
1				Black
2	Raw Value	Odd/Even?	Boolean Filter	Final Value
3	1	Odd	TRUE	1
4	2	Even	FALSE	
5	3	Odd	TRUE	3
6	4	Even	FALSE	
7	5	Odd	TRUE	5
8	6	Even	FALSE	

Figure 3-16. *The table that allows for chart filtering*

In column B, I use the following formula:

```
=CHOOSE(MOD(A3,2)+1,"Even","Odd")
```

So let's break this down.

Nested inside the CHOOSE conditional is the MOD( ) formula. MOD performs *modulo division*, which is a technical way of saying it performs division like a third grader. Remember when you first started learning how to divide, *3 divided by 2* would equal *1 remainder 1*? Well, modulo division performs this same operation but only returns the remainder part. In the case of MOD(A3,2) you're simply testing whether the list of numbers given in column A is odd or even. As you might recall, when even numbers are divided by two, there is never a remainder (think of it as a remainder of zero); for odd numbers there's always a remainder of one.

What you run into is that you're using the CHOOSE( ) formula to tell Excel whether to return the word "Odd," or to return the word "Even." CHOOSE( ), however, can't take in numbers that are less than one, and so far, it's possible this could return a zero. So, my solution is to add the one at the end. So going back to the original CHOOSE formula,

```
=CHOOSE(MOD(A3,2)+1,"Even","Odd")
```

...you can see how all the parts fit together.

Moving on to Column C (Figure 3-17), you're simply testing if the contents in Column are equal to the contents of your dropdown.

EXACT			▼	:	×	✓	*fx*	=(B3=$L$2)				
	A	B	C	D	E	F	G	H	I	J	K	L	M
1													
2	Raw Value	Odd/Even?	Boolean Filter	Final Value						Please Choose		Odd	
3	1	Odd	=(B3=$L$2)	1									
4	2	Even	FALSE							Odd			

Figure 3-17. *Testing whether the contents of the boolean filter are equal to the dropdown*

This is achieved by writing the following Boolean formula from cell C3:

```
=(B3=$L$2)
```

The parentheses surround the test condition telling Excel to either return a TRUE or FALSE value. When there's only one test case, the parentheses are optional. However, it's good practice to keep parentheses anyway, keeping in line with the idea presented above that you should match your formulas to manifest the conditions you're developing. And, specifically, note that the following two formulas are not equal:

```
=(B3=$L$2)+1   =\=   =B3=$L$2+1
```

Finally, in Column D you multiply columns A and C (Figure 3-18). When the number in Column A is multiplied by a TRUE value, it's the same as multiplying it by the number one. When multiplied by a FALSE value, it's the as multiplying it by zero. The chart is linked to column D so the outcomes in column D are automatically updated on the chart.

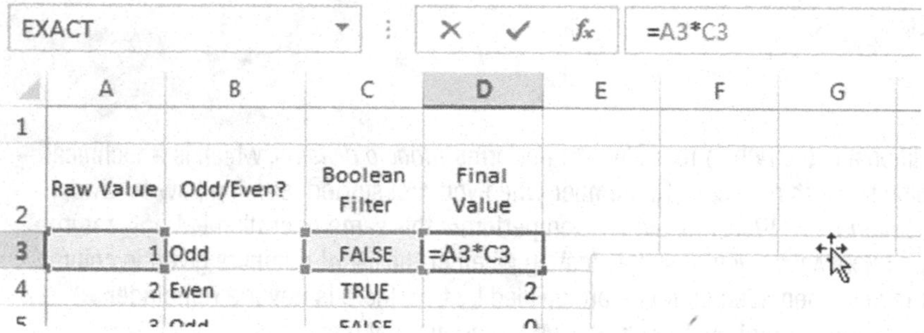

Figure 3-18. *The Final Value column of your table*

I have to admit: CHOOSE wasn't the best function for the example above. By all accounts, if you were thinking I should have used IF instead, you wouldn't have been off base. The values of "Even" and "Odd" aren't ordinal. Numbers are either only *even* or *odd*. And I'm usually of the belief that the more natural the function mirrors the problem, the easier it is to comprehend. What makes the example above such a good IF problem is because the Boolean dynamic, that TRUE/FALSE = 1/0, goes both ways. Recall in your test for an even or odd value, the MOD function was returning either a zero or a one. You could have written =CHOOSE(MOD(A3,2)+1,"Even","Odd") as =IF(MOD(A3,2),"Odd","Even") which is reasonably easier to read, and it's probably easier to comprehend when you come back to it later.

Condensing Your Work

What makes =IF(MOD(A3,2),"Odd","Even") so readable is because there are no nested conditions. Once you add more conditions, it becomes much harder to comprehend at first glance. And, when you represent information on your spreadsheet, you'll sometimes have to condense formulas from different cells into one to save space. In the example above, if you want to condense your work, you can do something like this in column D:

```
=IF(MOD(A3,2),IF($L$2="Odd",A3,0),IF($L$2="Even",A3,0))
```

But now the IF function is longer and harder to understand. Maybe it's time you dispense with the IF function altogether. But how can you recreate the same conditions without using IF? Well, you can use the exclusive-or function, XOR, like this:

```
=XOR($L$2="Even",MOD(A3,2))*A3
```

■ **Note** XOR is available only in Excel 2013.

The Legend of XOR( )-oh

Technically, XOR is not pronounced "zore," but rather as "ex-or," which as you've likely figured is shorthand for exclusive-or. So what the heck does XOR do? Well it's a type of truth-testing conditional function. You're probably somewhat familiar with Excel's cousin truth functions, AND and OR.

Let's review them first. AND tests if all the supplied conditional expressions are TRUE. If they are, AND returns TRUE. If one condition is not true, as in FALSE, AND returns FALSE. OR tests if *only one* argument is TRUE and returns TRUE when at least one conditional expression evaluates to TRUE. If all arguments passed to OR evaluate to FALSE, OR returns FALSE. Table 3-2 shows the outcomes for AND and OR formulas when supplied with only two arguments, x and y.

Table 3-2. *A Truth Table for AND and OR Functions*

X	Y	=AND(x,y)	=OR(x,y)
TRUE	TRUE	**TRUE**	**TRUE**
TRUE	FALSE	FALSE	**TRUE**
FALSE	TRUE	FALSE	**TRUE**
FALSE	FALSE	FALSE	FALSE

XOR adds an extra constraint: *only one of the arguments can contain a value of TRUE.* That's what makes it so *exclusive.* It's like a club where everyone is invited but only one person is allowed to come in—and that person is you, you lucky dog! You can think of OR as being *all inclusive* because it does not constrain the amount of TRUE values required to return TRUE. It's like a club that everyone can get into (but then everyone leaves because I decide to show up). The truth table is for XOR is shown in Table 3-3.

Table 3-3. *The Truth Table for XOR*

X	Y	=XOR(x,y)
TRUE	TRUE	FALSE
TRUE	FALSE	**TRUE**
FALSE	TRUE	**TRUE**
FALSE	FALSE	FALSE

Going back to your condensed formula, let's see how XOR( ) works by examining this formula:

```
=XOR($L$2="Even",MOD(A3,2))*A3.
```

Recall, MOD(A3,2) will return a one when A3 is odd and a zero when A3 is even. In the example above, you're always testing if the dropdown has "Even" selected. So, let's say A3 equals an odd value, like the number 3. Listing 3-6 shows a step-by-step evaluation when L2 is even. Listing 3-7 shows a step-by-step evaluation when L2 is odd.

Listing 3-6. Formula Evaluation When L2 Is Even

```
If $L$2="Even" then
=XOR($L$2="Even", MOD(A3,2))*A3
=XOR(TRUE, 1)*A3
=FALSE*A3
=0 * 3
=0
```

Listing 3-7. Formula Evaluation When L2 Is Odd

```
If $L$2="Odd" then
=XOR($L$2="Even", MOD(A3,2))*A3
=XOR(FALSE, 1)*A3
=TRUE*A3
=1 * 3
=3
```

So, think about this way: you're actually interested in the *inverse relationship* between your two conditions. If $L$2 has "Even" selected, for the value in A3 to show, it must also be even. For even values, MOD(A3,2) will return a zero (which is the opposite result of the test $L$2 = "Even"). If $L$2 has "Odd" selected, the first argument will return FALSE, but MOD(A3,2) will actually return a one.

Do We Really Need IF?

For this section, I'll combine everything you've learned so far to answer the question: do we really need IF? The fact is, many problems that feel like they need IF probably don't need it. Let's go through a few quick examples.

Need to test if a cell is blank so you can return a blank instead of a zero?

Use: =--REPT(A2, LEN(A2)>1)
Instead of: IF(LEN(A2) > 1, A2, "")
Note: "--" is shorthand to convert a string into a number.

Need to return a certain range based on a dropdown select?

Just add the numbers 1, 2, 3, and 4 to the beginning of your dropdown items (see Figure 3-19).

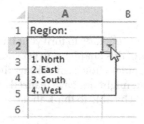

Figure 3-19. *Adding numbers to the dropdown items can help you quickly ascertain which item was selected without using an IF statement*

Use: =CHOOSE(--LEFT(A2, 1), NorthRange, EastRange, SouthRange, WestRange)
Instead of: IF(A2 = "North", NorthRange, IF(A2 = "East", EastRange,
                                    IF(A2 = "South", SouthRange, WestRange)

Want to know what grade you got?

Figure 3-20 shows a grade letter calculator.

	A	B
1	Final Score	69
2	Final Grade	D
3		
4	50	F
5	60	D
6	70	C
7	80	B
8	90	A
9		

Figure 3-20. *A grade calculator that uses INDEX and MATCH instead of nested IFs*

Use: =INDEX($B$4:$B$8, MATCH(B1,$A$4:$A$8,1))
Instead of: = IF(B1>89,"A",IF(B1>79,"B", IF(B1>69,"C",IF(B1>59,"D","F"))))

Need to return a -1 whenever a test condition is zero; otherwise return the value?

This example uses Figure 3-21 as an example.

	A	B	C	D	E	F
1	0	2	2	8	4	0
2	=-NOT(A1) + A1	2	2	8	4	-1

Figure 3-21. *You can use Boolean functions instead of IF*

Use: =-NOT(A1) + A1
Instead of: =IF(A1=0, A1, 0)

The Last Word

I realize some of the material in this chapter might be new for you. And perhaps you're not yet ready to turn your back on IF. Fair enough; although don't expect me to use it much from here on out! The point of this chapter is to get your mind to think differently about certain problems. IF is a common convention, but the popular choice isn't always the best. This chapter introduced you to formula concepts you've used many times before but might not have realized what they were or what they meant. Empowered with new knowledge, I'm confident you'll be able to think about formulas differently.

The best formulas fit somewhere on a spectrum of performance, readability, and design simplicity. If the formula you're using to model your problem feels like a *good fit*, chances are—it is. I firmly believe that formulas that are a natural fit to a problem give you that "intuitively pleasing" feeling when you look at them. If this chapter has you thinking how you might do some of your own formulas differently, then my work is done here (well, except for the other eight chapters coming your way).

CHAPTER 4

∎∎∎

Advanced Formula Concepts

The previous chapter's formula examples may have appeared complicated at first, but you should be able to use them with time, practice, and patience. If you followed the advice at the start of Chapter 3, which was to work through formulas with techniques like Excel's Evaluate Formula feature, you should find them easier to understand.

In this chapter, you will investigate how these formulas are applied. Specifically, I will cover the following:

- Filtering and highlighting

- Selection

- Aggregation

Filtering and Highlighting

Following what you learned about ones and zeros in Chapter 3, you can use formulas for filtering results. In Chapter 3, you employed a mechanism to filter even and odd values using Booleans. Highlighting, as it turns out, isn't much different than filtering. Let's take a look.

Filtering with Formulas

Figure 4-1 shows the tables I've set up for the example (download **Chapter4Ex1.xlsx** from the project files to follow along). If you have the example file open, we're starting on the tab, Project List (incomplete). Throughout the example files, tabs with the suffix "(incomplete)" will refer to the unfinished work we'll complete together. When available, tabs with the suffix "(complete)" will refer to completed versions I have built into the spreadsheet, so you can see what the final version looks like.

Please also make "Project List (incomplete)" look like the times I've mentioned worksheet tab names. On the left is the raw data. In the middle is the criteria that you want to filter, and on the right are some conditional tables to help know which items fit the criteria you would like to display. The information in the middle is linked to the Dashboard tab, which I'll get to in a moment.

	A	B	C	D	E	F	G	H I	J	K	L	M	N	O	P
1		Raw Data Table									Information Table				
2	Projects	NPV	Portfolio Risk	Project Lead				#	Projects	NPV	Portfolio Risk	Project Lead		Show on Front?	Index
3	Project A	11,894,611	Low	Larry		Selected		1	Project A	TRUE	TRUE	TRUE		TRUE	1
4	Project B	11,676,808	Med	Larry		NPV (>)	10,000,500	2	Project B	TRUE	FALSE	TRUE		FALSE	0
5	Project C	12,208,436	High	Larry		Portfolio Risk	Low	3	Project C	TRUE	FALSE	TRUE		FALSE	0
6	Project D	10,972,428	Low	Larry		Project Lead	Larry	4	Project D	TRUE	TRUE	TRUE		TRUE	4
7	Project E	10,439,155	High	Larry				5	Project E	TRUE	FALSE	TRUE		FALSE	0
8	Project F	10,080,330	High	Larry				6	Project F	TRUE	FALSE	TRUE		FALSE	0
9	Project G	11,080,632	Low	Barry				7	Project G	TRUE	TRUE	FALSE		FALSE	0
10	Project H	10,326,092	Low	Barry				8	Project H	TRUE	TRUE	FALSE		FALSE	0
11	Project I	10,215,675	Low	Barry				9	Project I	TRUE	TRUE	FALSE		FALSE	0
12	Project J	10,551,834	Low	Barry				#	Project J	TRUE	TRUE	FALSE		FALSE	0
13	Project K	11,941,962	Med	Barry				#	Project K	TRUE	FALSE	FALSE		FALSE	0
14	Project L	12,120,026	High	Barry				#	Project L	TRUE	FALSE	FALSE		FALSE	0
15	Project M	10,259,752	Low	Barry				#	Project M	TRUE	TRUE	FALSE		FALSE	0
16	Project N	10,253,060	Low	Barry				#	Project N	TRUE	TRUE	FALSE		FALSE	0
17	Project O	11,158,311	Low	Harry				#	Project O	TRUE	TRUE	FALSE		FALSE	0
18	Project P	10,703,286	Low	Harry				#	Project P	TRUE	TRUE	FALSE		FALSE	0
19	Project Q	10,736,631	Low	Larry				#	Project Q	TRUE	TRUE	TRUE		TRUE	17
20	Project R	11,508,068	High	Larry				#	Project R	TRUE	FALSE	TRUE		FALSE	0
21	Project S	10,524,512	High	Larry				#	Project S	TRUE	FALSE	TRUE		FALSE	0
22	Project T	10,162,742	Low	Larry				#	Project T	TRUE	TRUE	TRUE		TRUE	20
23															

Figure 4-1. *An example table to demonstrate applied formula concepts*

Let's take a better look at the table on the right. For the NPV column, let's set up a conditional to compare whether the selected NPV is greater than the item in the current row of the Raw Data Table (Figure 4-2).

EXACT			:	×	✓	*fx*	=(B3>ProjectList.NPV)

	A	B	C	D	E	F	G	H I	J	K	L
1		Raw Data Table								Information Table	
2	Projects	NPV	Portfolio Risk	Project Lead				#	Projects	NPV	Portfolio Risk	Pr
3	Project A	11,894,611	Low	Larry		Selected		1	Project A	=(B3>ProjectList.NPV)	
4	Project B	11,676,808	Med	Larry		NPV (>)	10,000,500	2	Project B	TRUE	FALSE
5	Project C	12,208,436	High	Larry		Portfolio Risk	Low	3	Project C	TRUE	FALSE
6	Project D	10,972,428	Low	Larry		Project Lead	Larry	4	Project D	TRUE	TRUE
7	Project E	10,439,155	High	Larry				5	Project E	TRUE	FALSE

Figure 4-2. *The Raw Data Table*

Then do the same comparisons for Portfolio Risk and Project Lead. See Figures 4-3 and 4-4.

EXACT			:	×	✓	*fx*	=(C3=ProjectList.PortfolioRisk)

	A	B	C	D	E	F	G	H I	J	K	L	M	N
1		Raw Data Table									Information Table		
2	Projects	NPV	Portfolio Risk	Project Lead				#	Projects	NPV	Portfolio Risk	Project Lead	Sh
3	Project A	11,894,611	Low	Larry		Selected		1	Project A	TRUE	=(C3=ProjectList.PortfolioRisk)	
4	Project B	11,676,808	Med	Larry		NPV (>)	10,000,500	2	Project B	TRUE	FALSE	TRUE
5	Project C	12,208,436	High	Larry		Portfolio Risk	Low	3	Project C	TRUE	FALSE	TRUE
6	Project D	10,972,428	Low	Larry		Project Lead	Larry	4	Project D	TRUE	TRUE	TRUE
7	Project F	10,439,155	High	Larry				5	Project F	TRUE	FALSE	TRUE

Figure 4-3. *You're testing for what level of Portfolio Risk is selected*

| EXACT | ▼ | : | × | ✓ | *fx* | =(D3=ProjectList.ProjectLead) |

▲	A	B	C	D	E	F	G	H	I	J	K	L	M	N	O
1		Raw Data Table										Information Table			
2	Projects	NPV	Portfolio Risk	Project Lead					#	Projects	NPV	Portfolio Risk	Project Lead		Show on Front?
3	Project A	11,894,611	Low	Larry			Selected		1	Project A	TRUE	TRUE	=(D3=ProjectList.ProjectLead)		
4	Project B	11,676,808	Med	Larry		NPV (>)	10,000,500		2	Project B	TRUE	FALSE	TRUE		FALSE
5	Project C	12,208,436	High	Larry		Portfolio Risk	Low		3	Project C	TRUE	FALSE	TRUE		FALSE
6	Project D	10,972,428	Low	Larry		Project Lead	Larry		4	Project D	TRUE	TRUE	TRUE		TRUE
7	Project E	10,438,155	High	Larry					5	Project E	TRUE	FALSE	TRUE		FALSE

Figure 4-4. *You're testing for which Project Lead has been selected*

In the last two columns, you identify which projects you want to be highlighted. Since you're looking for projects whose values come at the *intersection* of your criteria, you'll test if each condition is met, and you'll use AND for that (Figure 4-5).

I	J	K	L	M	N	O	
			Information Table				
:	Projects	NPV	Portfolio Risk	Project Lead		Show on Front?	Ir
1	Project A	TRUE	TRUE	TRUE		=AND(K3,L3,M3)	
2	Project B	TRUE	FALSE	TRUE		FALSE	

Figure 4-5. *Testing when all three conditions are met*

Finally, for extra help, you'll include the Project's index in column P. This isn't itself necessary to complete your work, but sometimes an extra column of information can help, provided you have enough room for it.

All of this work goes to help the highlighting mechanism developed on the Dashboard tab. Click the Dashboard (incomplete) tab in example file to see what I'm talking about (shown in Figure 4-6).

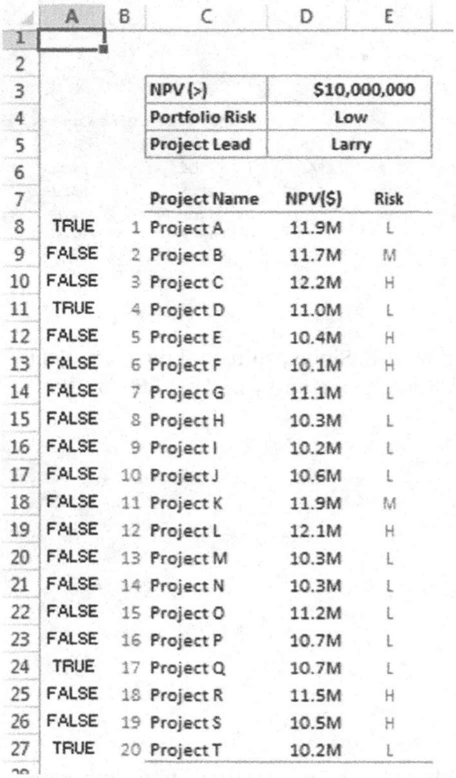

	A	B	C	D	E
1					
2					
3			NPV (>)	$10,000,000	
4			Portfolio Risk	Low	
5			Project Lead	Larry	
6					
7			Project Name	NPV($)	Risk
8	TRUE	1	Project A	11.9M	L
9	FALSE	2	Project B	11.7M	M
10	FALSE	3	Project C	12.2M	H
11	TRUE	4	Project D	11.0M	L
12	FALSE	5	Project E	10.4M	H
13	FALSE	6	Project F	10.1M	H
14	FALSE	7	Project G	11.1M	L
15	FALSE	8	Project H	10.3M	L
16	FALSE	9	Project I	10.2M	L
17	FALSE	10	Project J	10.6M	L
18	FALSE	11	Project K	11.9M	M
19	FALSE	12	Project L	12.1M	H
20	FALSE	13	Project M	10.3M	L
21	FALSE	14	Project N	10.3M	L
22	FALSE	15	Project O	11.2M	L
23	FALSE	16	Project P	10.7M	L
24	TRUE	17	Project Q	10.7M	L
25	FALSE	18	Project R	11.5M	H
26	FALSE	19	Project S	10.5M	H
27	TRUE	20	Project T	10.2M	L

Figure 4-6. *The Dashboard (incomplete) tab*

Now take a look at Column A. Column A tests whether the current index in Column B is the same as the index returned from the Project List tab. Essentially, the result is the same as the Show on Front field in Column O on the Project List tab (Figure 4-7).

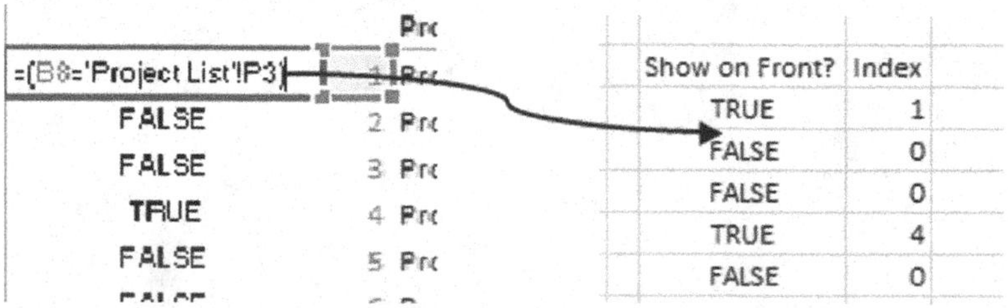

	Pro		Show on Front?	Index
=(B8='Project List'!P3)	1 Pro		TRUE	1
FALSE	2 Pro		FALSE	0
FALSE	3 Pro		FALSE	0
TRUE	4 Pro		TRUE	4
FALSE	5 Pro		FALSE	0
FALSE	6 P			

Figure 4-7. *TRUE/FALSE on the dashboard corresponds to backend calculations*

Conditional Highlighting Using Formulas

In this section, I'll talk about how to add condition highlighting to the spreadsheet. Let's do the following steps.

1. Highlight the project table, as I have done in Figure 4-8 by selecting cells C8:C27.

		Project Name	NPV($)	Risk
TRUE	1	Project A	11.9M	L
FALSE	2	Project B	11.7M	M
FALSE	3	Project C	12.2M	H
TRUE	4	Project D	11.0M	L
FALSE	5	Project E	10.4M	H
FALSE	6	Project F	10.1M	H
FALSE	7	Project G	11.1M	L
FALSE	8	Project H	10.3M	L
FALSE	9	Project I	10.2M	L
FALSE	10	Project J	10.6M	L
FALSE	11	Project K	11.9M	M
FALSE	12	Project L	12.1M	H
FALSE	13	Project M	10.3M	L
FALSE	14	Project N	10.3M	L
FALSE	15	Project O	11.2M	L
FALSE	16	Project P	10.7M	L
TRUE	17	Project Q	10.7M	L
FALSE	18	Project R	11.5M	H
FALSE	19	Project S	10.5M	H
TRUE	20	Project T	10.2M	L

Figure 4-8. *Selecting cells C8:C27*

2. From the Home tab, go to Conditional Formatting ➤ New Rule ➤ Use a formula to determine which cells to format.

3. Click in the address box titled Format Values where this formula is true. In the formula box, type =(and then click on cell A8, which is the top of the condition list.

4. A8 will appear as the absolute reference $A$8. However, you do not want every row to test only this cell. Rather, you want each row to test against the cell for the row. So press F4 twice to toggle through the absolute reference options until you reach $A8. Then finish the formula by typing =TRUE). Figure 4-9 shows the correct formula.

Figure 4-9. *The Edit Formatting Rule dialog box*

5. Click the Format button. Under the Font tab, select Bold under Font Style. In the Color
    dropdown, select the Black color to change the selection from Automatic. On the Fill tab,
    choose a light color to serve as the filtered item's background. I've chosen a light peach
    color. Finally, press OK in each dialog box until you've returned to the spreadsheet.

If you've performed these steps correctly, you should see several items highlighted in your list (see Figure 4-10).
To bring more emphasis to these items—and to deemphasize the items outside your selection—highlight the table
range again, C8:C27, and set the font to a gray color that is lighter than black but still readable. I chose the darkest
gray at the bottom of the first color column. Finally, you'll want to get rid of those conditional formulas in Column A.
The easiest way to do this is to hide the entire column by right-clicking Column A and selecting Hide. Alternatively,
I've simply set the font of the condition formulas to white. Personally, I like having the extra margin of white space
on the left side of the screen.

		Project Name	NPV($)	Risk
7		**Project Name**	**NPV($)**	**Risk**
8	1	Project A	11.9M	L
9	2	Project B	11.7M	M
10	3	**Project C**	**12.2M**	**H**
11	4	Project D	11.0M	L
12	5	**Project E**	**10.4M**	**H**
13	6	**Project F**	**10.1M**	**H**
14	7	Project G	11.1M	L
15	8	Project H	10.3M	L
16	9	Project I	10.2M	L
17	10	Project J	10.6M	L
18	11	Project K	11.9M	M
19	12	Project L	12.1M	H
20	13	Project M	10.3M	L
21	14	Project N	10.3M	L
22	15	Project O	11.2M	L
23	16	Project P	10.7M	L
24	17	Project Q	10.7M	L
25	18	**Project R**	**11.5M**	**H**
26	19	**Project S**	**10.5M**	**H**
27	20	Project T	10.2M	L
28				

Figure 4-10. *A list of highlighted items*

One last thought before moving on: I could have created another conditional format formula testing if A8=FALSE and then colored everything gray based on that. To me, that's extra work. Conditional formats are volatile actions. Consider this: no instruction is executed to set the table items that are FALSE to be grayed out if you've already set them to gray by default. Remember to always be on the lookout for shortcuts.

Selecting

Selection is the process of returning only certain information (thinking of selecting from a group). Selecting is similar to filtering and highlighting, except that selecting only returns the information you're interested in. Filtering, for example, simply hides the information you're not interested in. Highlighting does the same as filtering through emphasizing and deemphasizing certain items. Selection, on the other hand, always contains **only** the complete set of information you're interested in. Nothing more or less.

Open example file Chapter4Ex2.xlsx. In this example, you're going to create a range that can grow and shrink dynamically based on what you want to return. In this way, you'll be creating the mechanism that selects the portion to return. Go to the Project List tab, and note the column of zeros you've created, as shown in Figure 4-11.

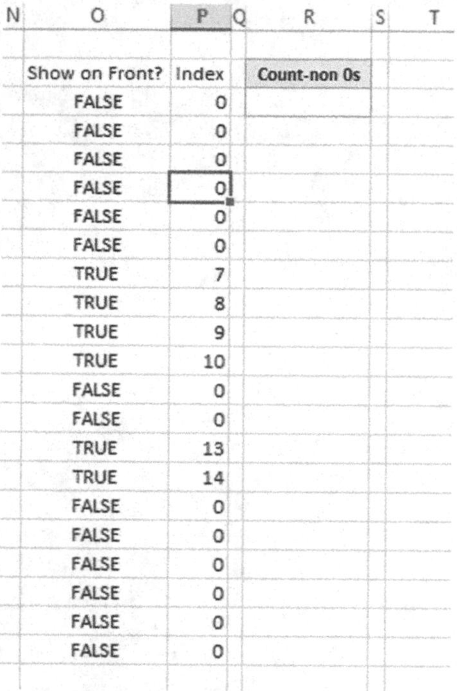

Show on Front?	Index	Count-non 0s
FALSE	0	
FALSE	0	
FALSE	0	
FALSE	0	
FALSE	0	
FALSE	0	
TRUE	7	
TRUE	8	
TRUE	9	
TRUE	10	
FALSE	0	
FALSE	0	
TRUE	13	
TRUE	14	
FALSE	0	
FALSE	0	
FALSE	0	
FALSE	0	
FALSE	0	
FALSE	0	

Figure 4-11. *The Project List tab*

If you recall from the previous chapter, the zeros indicate projects you don't want to return. Alternatively, the numbers indicate projects you DO want to return. So, what you need to do now is count those projects. I've already laid out a spot for this count in cell R3. So go ahead and put this formula into R3:

```
=COUNTIF($P$3:$P$22,">0")
```

In the columns next to the box labeled Count-non 0s, set up the column headers as I have in Figure 4-12.

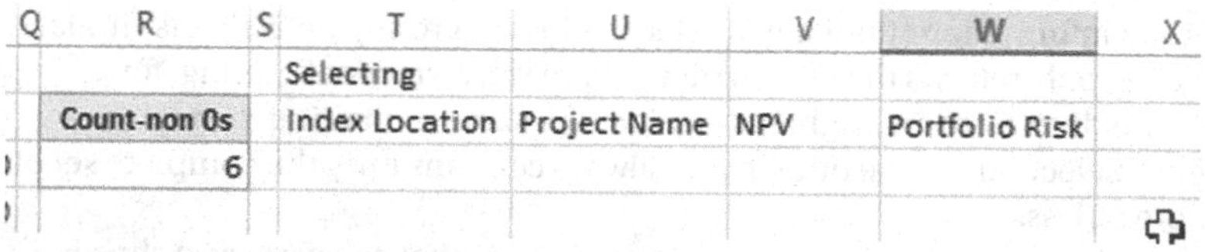

	Count-non 0s		Selecting Index Location	Project Name	NPV		Portfolio Risk	
	6							

Figure 4-12. *Column headers that you will use in the process of developing a selecting mechansim*

Now, follow these steps.

1. In cell T3, type in the following formula (shown in Figure 4-13):

   =LARGE($P$3:$P$22,I3)

	#	Projects	NPV	Portfolio Risk	Project Lead	Show on Front?	Index	Count-non 0s	Selecting Index Location	Project
	1	Project A	TRUE	TRUE	FALSE	FALSE	0	6	=LARGE($P$3:$P$22,I3)	

Figure 4-13. Using the LARGE function in the Index location

Note what what's happening here. You're using the index you created in column I to pull out the nth largest value from within the range indices that aren't zero. When you drag down, you'll have grouped all the indices you're interested in at the top of the range (Figure 4-14). You should find there are six non-zero items at the top—exactly as the formula predicted.

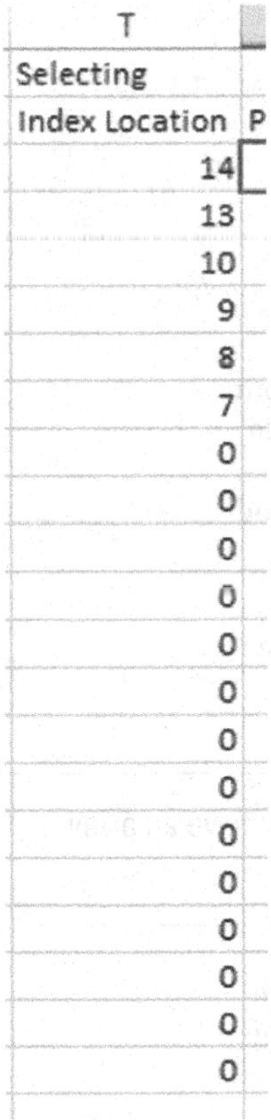

T Selecting Index Location	P
14	
13	
10	
9	
8	
7	
0	
0	
0	
0	
0	
0	
0	
0	
0	
0	
0	
0	
0	
0	

Figure 4-14. The LARGE function returns the indices of the items you're interested in at the top of the range

2. Now, in cell U3, type =INDEX($A$3:$B$22,T3,), as shown in Figure 4-15.

	A	B	C	D	S	T	U	V	W
1		Raw Data Table				Selecting			
2	Projects	NPV	Portfolio Risk	Project Lead		Index Location	Project Name	NPV	
3	Project A	11,894,611	Low	Larry		14	=INDEX($A$3:$B$22,T3,)		
4	Project B	11,676,808	Med	Larry		13			
5	Project C	12,208,436	High	Larry		10			
6	Project D	10,972,428	Low	Larry		9			
7	Project E	10,439,155	High	Larry		8			
8	Project F	10,080,330	High	Larry		7			
9	Project G	11,080,632	Low	Barry		0			
10	Project H	10,326,092	Low	Barry		0			
11	Project I	10,215,675	Low	Barry		0			
12	Project J	10,551,834	Low	Barry		0			
13	Project K	11,941,962	Med	Barry		0			
14	Project L	12,120,026	High	Barry		0			
15	Project M	10,259,752	Low	Barry		0			
16	Project N	10,253,060	Low	Barry		0			
17	Project O	11,158,311	Low	Harry		0			
18	Project P	10,703,286	Low	Harry		0			
19	Project Q	10,736,631	Low	Larry		0			
20	Project R	11,508,068	High	Larry		0			
21	Project S	10,524,512	High	Larry		0			
22	Project T	10,162,742	Low	Larry		0			
23									

Figure 4-15. Adding the INDEX formula to the Project Name column

3. When you press Enter you should immediately get a #VALUE! error. But don't worry about that for now. Using the cell anchor in the lower right of the selected cell, drag the formula over to V3 to copy it into that cell. Now, with both U3 and V3 selected, click the formula bar and press Ctrl+Shift+Enter. You should see a full row returned of the project name and NPV values. Now drag down.

In case you're wondering why you need to do this, remember that INDEX allows you to return one or more cells from within an array; all you must supply are the row(s) or columns(s) you'd like to grab. Because you returned more than a single cell, you had to use Ctrl+Shift+Enter.

■ **Note** Remember, any time you return more than a single cell, you have an array formula. When you have an array formula, you must use Ctrl+Shift+Enter.

---

4. Now for some fun! You're going to use a dynamic range formula you learned about in the previous chapter. Remember, dynamic ranges requires two things: (a) a contiguous range; and (b) the total amount of items in the range. Luckily, the first thing you did was create that count of non-zeros!

In a cell off to the side (I've chosen X3), type =OFFSET($V$3,0,0,$R$3), as shown in Figure 4-16.

Q	R	S	T	U	V	W	X	Y	Z
		Selecting							
ex	Count-non 0s		Index Location	Project Name	NPV				
0	6		14	Project N	10253060		=OFFSET($V$3,0,0,$R$3)		
0			13	Project M	10259752				

Figure 4-16. Using OFFSET to create a dynamic side function

Remember how OFFSET works. That fourth argument specifies the height of the offset range to be returned. Here, you don't actually want the returned range to be moved from cell V3 (which is why you supply a zero in the first two arguments); you simply want V3 to be the starting point and to have the range "grow" (or expand) downward from there.

5. When you press Enter, the result returned should be the same value as in V3. If you drag X3's anchor downward, you should see all six values returned, and you'll start getting errors thereafter. At this point, you're simply testing the formula. Now that you know it works, you're going to assign it to a named range.

So, click on X3 and copy the formula now that you know it's working. Go to Name Manager from the Formulas tab. Click on New. Give it a name like "ProjectList.ReturnSelection" and paste the formula you copied into the Refers To box. Press OK until you're back at the spreadsheet screen.

6. Go to the dashboard worksheet.

7. From the Insert tab, insert a column chart. If the chart automatically selects data, right-click the chart and go to Select Data and remove any preloaded data.

8. Now, click the Add button and press OK for whatever default data is loaded. Series1 with a value of 1 should be the only series in the Select Data dialog, as shown in Figure 4-17.

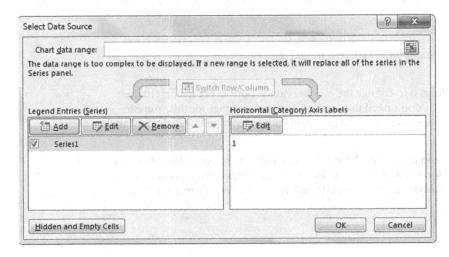

Figure 4-17. The Select Data Source dialog box

9. Click OK to return to the spreadsheet. Now click the single column displayed to see its formula in the formula bar.

10. Now you're going to replace the "{1}" with a reference to the named range you just created. For this series, *you must include the workbook name,* as shown in Figure 4-18, otherwise this mechanism won't work. Why? Not sure: that's just what Excel wants. I don't ask questions.

```
=SERIES(,,'Chapter 10 Ex3 .xlsx'!ProjectList.ReturnSelection,1)
```

Figure 4-18. *The SERIES function that appears when you click on a chart*

Viola! If it worked correctly, you should see a series of columns like in Figure 4-19.

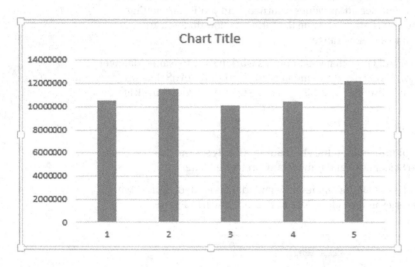

Figure 4-19. *A dynamic chart that is automatically linked to your data selections*

11. The last step you'll perform is to change the numbers at the bottom of the chart to their correct labels. You actually don't need to create a new dynamic range for this. You can simply supply an entire range of labels and Excel will know to only pull back the top labels automatically.

To see what I'm talking about, right-click the chart again and go to Select Data. Press the Edit button under the Horizontal category. Select the entire range of projects in column U from the Project List worksheet and press OK until you reach the spreadsheet screen (Figure 4-20).

S	T	U	V	W	X	Y	Z	AA
	Selecting							
	Index Location	Project Name	NPV					
	19	Project S	10524512					
	18	Project R	1					
	6	Project F	1					
	5	Project E	1					
	3	Project C	1					
	0	Project A	1					
	0	Project A	1					
	0	Project A	11894611					
	0	Project A	11894611					
	0	Project A	11894611					

Axis Labels dialog: Axis label range: ='Project List (incomplete)'!$U$3:$ = Project S, Pro... [OK] [Cancel]

Figure 4-20. *The Axis Labels selection box*

Now the labels are automatically assigned! Go ahead and mess with the dropdown boxes to see it work in action.

Okay, one last piece before moving on. Go ahead and click one of those columns again in the chart and look at the formula bar. You should see that the range you've entered for your labels is now the second argument in the formula box. Just like for the series values, you could have simply entered the label range directly in the formula box. In case you're interested, here's how the series formula breaks down:

=SERIES(*series_title* , *series_label_range* , *series_value_range* , *series_index*)

If you'd like to supply this chart a title directly, go ahead and type a string into that series_title parameter. That last parameter, series_index, holds the current index of the series. If you have multiple series in your chart, setting the series_index will change the series order by inserting the series you're currently editing at the index you give.

Aggregating

In this section, I'll talk about aggregation, particularly the formulas you can use for aggregation. I'll also take a detour into some algebra, but nothing terrible. I promise.

Using SUMPRODUCT for Aggregation

Aggregation is the process of grouping similar items and presenting them as a whole. Excel has several aggregation formulas that you might already use every day including SUM, AVERAGE, and COUNT. If you want to get even more complicated—as if life isn't already complicated enough!—you could use the SUMIF/SUMIFS functions or COUNTIF/COUNTIFS functions to find the sum and count of multiple ranges of the same length satisfying certain criteria.

Let's say for the information in Figure 4-21, you were interested in all projects by Larry or Barry in which NPV is greater than 11,000,000 *or* portfolio risk is low.

⁄	A	B	C	D
1		Raw Data Table		
2	Projects	NPV	Portfolio Ris	Project Lead
3	Project A	11,894,611	Low	Larry
4	Project B	11,676,808	Med	Larry
5	Project C	12,208,436	High	Larry
6	Project D	10,972,428	Low	Larry
7	Project E	10,439,155	High	Larry
8	Project F	10,080,330	High	Larry
9	Project G	11,080,632	Low	Barry
10	Project H	10,326,092	Low	Barry
11	Project I	10,215,675	Low	Barry
12	Project J	10,551,834	Low	Barry
13	Project K	11,941,962	Med	Barry
14	Project L	12,120,026	High	Barry
15	Project M	10,259,752	Low	Barry
16	Project N	10,253,060	Low	Barry
17	Project O	11,158,311	Low	Harry
18	Project P	10,703,286	Low	Harry
19	Project Q	10,736,631	Low	Larry
20	Project R	11,508,068	High	Larry
21	Project S	10,524,512	High	Larry
22	Project T	10,162,742	Low	Larry

Figure 4-21. *The Raw Data table containing projects, NPV, portfolio risk, and the project's lead*

To do that, you could use this formula, which isn't very pretty:

```
=COUNTIFS(ProjectLead,"Larry",NPV,">11000000")+COUNTIFS(ProjectLead,"Larry",PortfolioRisk,"Low")+
COUNTIFS(ProjectLead,"Barry",NPV,">11000000")+COUNTIFS(ProjectLead,"Barry",PortfolioRisk,"Low")
```

This is because SUMIFS and COUNTIFS test for the intersection of data by themselves. There's no room for an OR condition in these formulas. But you have alternatives. For example, you could use the SUMPRODUCT formula for this problem, which would look like this:

```
=SUMPRODUCT((((ProjectLead="Larry")+(ProjectLead="Barry"))*((NPV>11000000)+(PortfolioRisk="Low"))))
```

I know you're scratching your head, so let's dig deeper. SUMPRODUCT by its name suggests it was designed for matrix algebra operations. To wit, Microsoft's definition of SUMPRODUCT is pretty mathematical. Specifically, SUMPRODUCT "multiplies corresponding components in the given arrays, and returns the *sum* of those products" (my emphasis). But this exactly what's so great about SUMPRODUCT.

When you write something like (ProjectLead="Barry") you're turning the range given by ProjectLead into array of TRUE/FALSE based on the supplied condition. That's from Chapter 3. So something like (ProjectLead="Larry")*(NPV>11000000) is calculated as shown in Figure 4-22.

L	M	N	O	P	Q	R	S	T	U	V
(ProjectLead="Larry")*(NPV>11000000)				Dot Product Calculation						
Project Lead		NPV		Project Lead		NPV		Result		
Larry		11,894,611		1	*	1		1		
Larry		11,676,808		1	*	1		1		
Larry		12,208,436		1	*	1		1		
Larry		10,972,428		1	*	0		0		
Larry		10,439,155		1	*	0		0		
Larry		10,080,330		1	*	0		0		
Barry		11,080,632		0	*	1		0		
Barry		10,326,092		0	*	0		0		
Barry	*	10,215,675	=	0	*	0	=	0	=	4
Barry		10,551,834		0	*	0		0		
Barry		11,941,962		0	*	1		0		
Barry		12,120,026		0	*	1		0		
Barry		10,259,752		0	*	0		0		
Barry		10,253,060		0	*	0		0		
Harry		11,158,311		0	*	1		0		
Harry		10,703,286		0	*	0		0		
Larry		10,736,631		1	*	0		0		
Larry		11,508,068		1	*	1		1		
Larry		10,524,512		1	*	0		0		
Larry		10,162,742		1	*	0		0		

Figure 4-22. *A visual represetation of what's happening when you use SUMPRODUCT*

In a certain sense, you're performing a query on the data. If you know SQL, the arrangement above could also be written as

```
SELECT COUNT(ProjectLead)
WHERE ProjectLead = "Larry" AND NPV > 11000000
```

You're About To Be FOILed!

OK, I know what you're thinking, *how the heck am I ever going to remember how to write one of those fancy* SUMPRODUCT *formulas?* Well, it all comes down to FOILing, which you might recall from your early days of learning algebra.

At first glance, the series of COUNTIFS functions appears easier to write and understand, even if the formula ends up being much longer. But I'm here to tell you that if you can write a series of COUNTIFS functions, you're already writing the same formula. No, seriously: I can prove this to you with some simple algebra. So let's talk FOILing (First, Outside, Inside, Last) from your algebra class. Let's do it on an expression inside the SUMPRODUCT formula.

So

```
((ProjectLead="Larry")+(ProjectLead="Barry"))*((NPV>11000000)+(PortfolioRisk="Low"))
=
    (ProjectLead="Larry")*(NPV>11000000)
+   (ProjectLead="Larry")*(PortfolioRisk="Low")
+   (ProjectLead="Barry")*(NPV>11000000)
+   (ProjectLead="Barry")*(PortfolioRisk="Low")
```

Now compare that FOILed expression to series of COUNTIFS functions.

```
=
    COUNTIFS(ProjectLead,"Larry",NPV,">11000000")
+   COUNTIFS(ProjectLead,"Larry",PortfolioRisk,"Low")
+   COUNTIFS(ProjectLead,"Barry",NPV,">11000000")
+   COUNTIFS(ProjectLead,"Barry",PortfolioRisk,"Low")
```

Here's the kicker: the plus symbol (+) acts as your OR condition and the multiplication symbol acts as your AND condition. If you think you'll have trouble remember the plus's + and multiplication's *, remember that these symbols aren't arbitrary, they represent algebraic operations.

■ **Note**   Remember, for SUMPRODUCT queries, + = OR, * = AND.

If you open Chapter4Ex3, I've placed a summary table on the front page that employs SUMPRODUCT (Figure 4-23).

Project Breakdown

	NPV		
	<11M	>12.0M	
High	=SUMPRODUCT((NPVRange<11000000)*(ProjectList.PortfolioRiskRange='Dashboard (incomplete)'!$G21))		
Med	0	0	
Low	9	0	
	12	2	

Figure 4-23. A demonstration of SUMPRODUCT on your dashboard

Reusable Components

In this section, I'll take a few moments to go through a concept I call *reusable components*. Take a look at the outlined components in Figure 4-24.

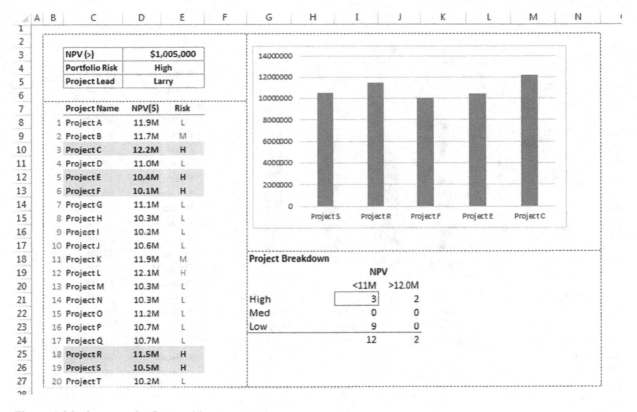

Figure 4-24. *An example of reusable componants*

Admittedly, these components were not placed with any specific care. I did this on purpose to demonstrate how easily these components can be moved around, as shown in Figure 4-25.

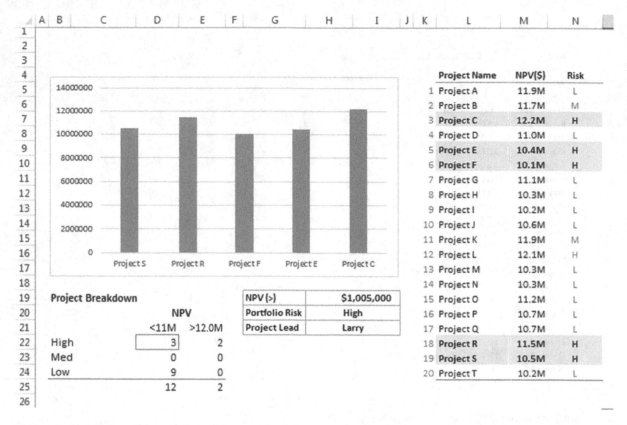

Figure 4-25. *A demonstration of how componants can be easily moved around*

There was some reformatting required, of course. But if I select the entire region of a table, I'm able to move it somewhere else on the screen without having to update any code or other formulas that refer that area. In addition, if I want to create another table similar to the one above, I can copy and paste the table into another free area on the spreadsheet and update the formulas that make it refer to another desired location. This is what is meant by *reusability*. And developing reusable components really helps down the road. We'll return to this idea several times before the book ends.

The Last Word

In this chapter, you build upon the formulas presented in the previous chapter. You applied what you learned to create the processes of filtering, highlighting, selecting, and aggregation. Finally, you learned about the usefulness of reusable components. In the next chapter, I'll talk about working in form controls.

CHAPTER 5

■■■

Working with Form Controls

When introducing controls, I like to use my own technical definition. Specifically, form controls are the *whiz bangs*, *doodads*, *whatchamacallits*, and *thingamajigs* that give your spreadsheet enhanced interactivity. You may know them by their street names: check boxes, scroll bars, labels, etc. Figure 5-1 shows a group of controls lounging about in their natural habitat, the Excel spreadsheet.

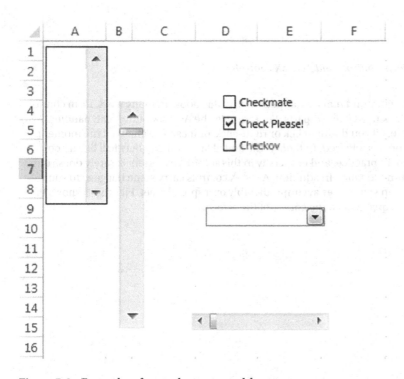

Figure 5-1. *Examples of controls on a spreadsheet*

Welcome to the Control Room

Excel contains two types of controls you can use on your spreadsheets. The first are form controls, and they are the subject of this chapter. The second are ActiveX controls, which we won't deal with in this book. There are significant differences between the two types of controls; however, they're both located in the same Insert box button, in the Controls group on the Developer tab. One important difference worth noting is that form controls are always on top, ActiveX controls are always on the bottom (see Figure 5-2).

Figure 5-2. *The dropdown menu showing form controls and ActiveX controls*

Let's take a moment to discuss why ActiveX won't make an appearance in this book. In many ways, form controls are leaner, more lightweight versions of their ActiveX counterparts. For example, the ActiveX button can handle several different types of click events. It can test if you double-click or right-click, or it can fire an event the moment your mouse button is pressed down but before it's released. In theory, the added functionality may feel like a boon of capabilities has been dumped on your lap. In practice, and especially in this author's experience, rarely does your spreadsheet require that level of advanced functionality. In addition, ActiveX controls carry some baggage to your memory usage and file size; moreover, they can sometimes act unpredictably on a spreadsheet. Figure 5-3 shows the Slider Bar control acting up by appearing unexpectedly in the corner of the screen.

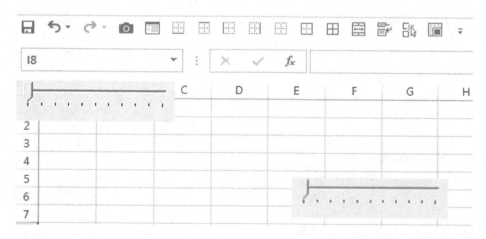

Figure 5-3. *A very common ActiveX issue: the Slider ActiveX control appears in both the upper-left side of the sheet and its initial location on the spreadsheet*

Form controls, on the other hand, are much more lightweight. However, they are also much more limited in what they can do, at least compared to their ActiveX cousins. And, unlike ActiveX controls, form controls can do a lot without any VBA. In fact, this is one of the reasons I love form controls. Following the ideas presented in Chapter 2, if you don't need to use VBA, you shouldn't. Below, I begin with the fundamentals of form controls and present a few examples that will serve as reusable components continuing throughout the book.

Form Control Fundamentals

Think of form controls as simply an extension of the formulas you learned how to use in previous chapters. Those formulas relied strongly on the spreadsheet for the storage and manipulation of values. Figure 5-4 shows an interactive legend that lets the user check "on" and "off" for which series they want to view.

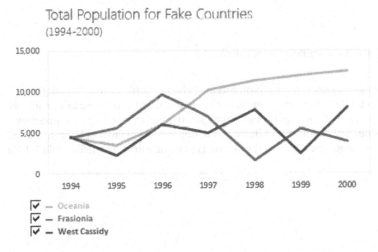

Figure 5-4. *An interactive legend using the form control CheckBox*

Behind this interactive legend is the form control CheckBox. The CheckBox links to a cell location that either results in a TRUE or FALSE depending on whether the check box is selected or not. (TRUE = selected; FALSE = not selected.) Since TRUE and FALSE are equal to 1 and 0, you can use these response values in a formula to change the data behind the chart. When the CheckBox is deselected, you do some work behind the scenes to change the number the series data to something that won't appear on the chart (see Figure 5-5).

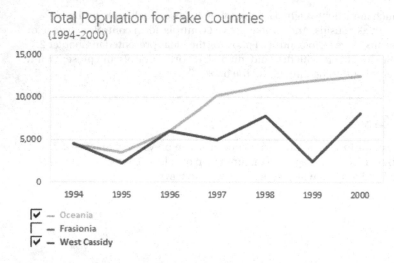

Figure 5-5. *When the check box is deselected, the line disappears from the chart*

I'll talk more about how to do something like this later in the chapter in the "The Dynamic Legend" section.

As you can see from Figure 5-6, there are a total of ten form controls to choose from. Three of those form controls are grayed out. Those controls will always be grayed out for insertion into the spreadsheet. In fact, the only time they are ever available is for Excel 4.0 Macros, an older technology that Microsoft has deprecated in favor of UserForms and ActiveX controls. Officially, Excel 4.0 Macros are no longer supported so I won't spend any time on them. Table 5-1 list all the form controls to insert.

Figure 5-6. *The Form Controls dropdown showing controls that are available to insert onto the spreadsheet*

Table 5-1. *Form Control Descriptions*

Name	Icon	Description
Button		Button inserts a gray button onto your spreadsheet. You can assign a macro to be executed when the button is clicked.
ComboBox		The ComboBox is similar to the data validation dropdown you can do in a cell. You can supply the ComboBox a list of data from your spreadsheet. The ComboBox will create a dropdown from which to choose a selected item from that list.
CheckBox		The CheckBox inserts a box onto your spreadsheet that you can toggle to be checked or unchecked. You can link a CheckBox to a cell to have it display TRUE or FALSE based on whether it's checked or not.
Spinner		The Spinner allows you to insert Up and Down paddles on your spreadsheet. You can link the Spinner to a cell such that when you press up, the cell value increases, and when you press down, the cell value decreases.
ListBox		A ListBox is similar to a ComboBox. However, instead of a dropdown, the ListBox shows a larger list of items that users can scroll through.
Option Button		The Option Button is similar to the CheckBox. However, groups of Option Buttons are mutually exclusive. That means only one Option Button can be selected at a time, while no such constraints exist on Checkboxes. Similar to Checkboxes, you can link Option Buttons directly to a cell.
GroupBox		A GroupBox has no real interactivity but can surround other controls to create delineation and flow.
Label	*Aa*	A Label is a simple textbox that can be placed anywhere on a sheet. Labels are a bit limited compared to Excel's native text boxes.
Scroll Bar		The Scroll Bar is similar to the Spinner except the Scroll Bar has an area in the middle in which you can drag the value up or down. But similar to the Spinner, you can link the Scroll Bar to a cell and use the up and down (and drag) paddles to change the cell's value.

Next, we're going to go through my favorite controls. I call them my favorite because of the entire bunch, I believe they're the most useful. After we go through my favorites, we'll go through my least favorites—the ones I believe you should avoid in favor of better alternatives available.

The ComboBox Control

The ComboBox control is a useful mechanism that essentially mimics the behavior of a data validation dropdown list. But there is a difference between the two that is worth noting. Figure 5-7 shows a data validation dropdown both when a selection is being made (that is, the cell is active) and when no selection is being made.

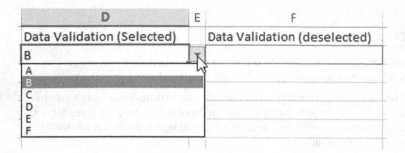

Figure 5-7. On the left, the validation list dropdown is expanded. On the right, the cell has been deselected

Now compare the aesthetics of the data validation dropdown in Figure 5-7 to the form control ComboBox list in Figure 5-8.

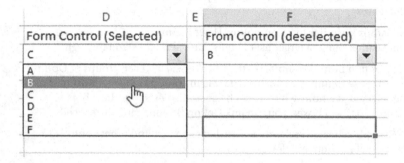

Figure 5-8. On the left, the form control dropdown is expanded. On the right, the form control has been deseltected

Notice the different aesthetics between the two "dropdown" lists. Generally, validation lists are better when you have a column of cells and each cell contains a dropdown, since the dropdown arrow won't appear in every cell, making for a clean appearance.

To view any control's properties, select the control and press the Properties button in the Controls group on the Developer tab shown in Figure 5-9—or, right-click a control, select Format Control, and select the Control tab.

Figure 5-9. The Properties Button in the Controls group on the Developer tab

Figure 5-10 shows the Format Control dialog box for the ComboBox control. In this dialog box, you can change various aspects of the form control from the Control tab.

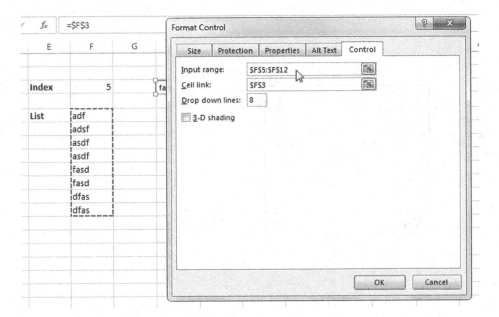

Figure 5-10. *The Format Control properties dialog box*

Note that you have two fields you can connect to the spreadsheet. The Input Range field allows you to select a desired range to fill the dropdown. The Cell link field allows you to specify a cell to display the index of the selected item.

The ListBox Control

The ListBox control is similar to the ComboBox control in that it also uses the Input range and Cell link fields. However, I believe you can better employ several mechanisms incorporated in the ListBox control, including creating a scrollable list (see Figure 5-11).

▲	A	B	C	D	E
1					
2		**List**			
3		Jordan			
4		Stephen			
5		Melissa			
6		Katherine			
7		Josh			
8		Nick			
9		Nigel			
10		Tom			
11		Nora			
12		Sydney			
13		Lauren			
14		Marsha			
15		Randy			

Figure 5-11. *The ListBox control contains a scrollable list of elements pulled from the spreadsheet*

One reason I prefer the ListBox control to the ComboBox is because I want to be able to see the data all at once. Moreover, as you'll see when you use the ComboBox, you can make the size of the control however large you want. But no matter how big that dropdown arrow becomes, the control's font and selection list underneath will always stay the same. Figure 5-12 shows a particularly egregious example. Rather than fooling the viewer with these strange aesthetics, you're better off sticking to ListBox.

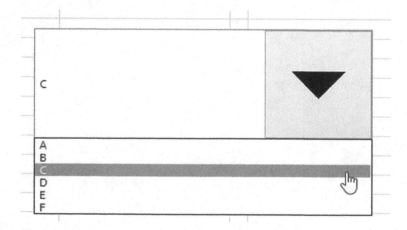

Figure 5-12. *The combo box is sized much larger than it ever should be*

The Scroll Bar Control

The Scroll Bar is amazing and probably my favorite form control. It's simple but powerful. The basic idea is that you can link the scroll bar's value to any available cell on a spreadsheet. I've done just this in Figure 5-13. As the scroll paddle (that's the gray bar between the upper and lower paddles) increases, so does the value in C2. Similarly, as it decreases, the value in C2 decreases.

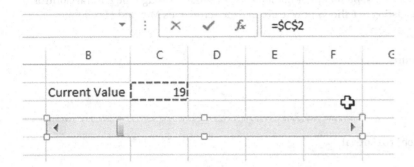

Figure 5-13. *A form control Scroll Bar linked to the cell C2*

The form control Scroll Bar contains some other great properties, as shown in Figure 5-14.

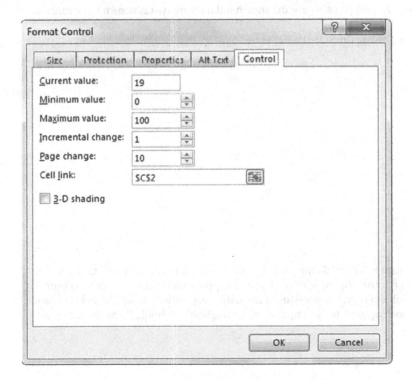

Figure 5-14. *The Format Control dialog box for the Scroll Bar*

Note that the Cell link field refers to same location in the formula bar in Figure 5-13. In Figure 5-14, you can see that the form control Scroll Bar comes with many more field properties than the ComboBox and ListBox controls. You can use the Minimum Value and Maximum Value fields to set the upper and lower bounds of the scroll bar. Indeed, you'll be doing just that in later chapters of this book. You can also use the Incremental Change field to set how much the value increases or decreases when you press the scroll bar's paddle. Finally, the Page change field refers to how much of an increase or decrease occurs when you click into the scroll bar itself and not on a upper or lower paddle.

Note that only one of the text fields in the Format Control dialog box (see Figure 5-14) can directly tie to a cell–the Cell link. The other fields shown in Figure 5-14 must be set either manually by a human (through the Format Control dialog box) or programmatically with code. Listing 5-1 shows how to change the scroll bar's Min and Max fields through code.

Listing 5-1. The SetScrollBarLimits Procedure

```
Public Sub SetScrollBarLimits()
    Const MAX_VAL = 20
    Const MIN_VAL = 3

    With Me.Shapes("Scroll Bar 1").ControlFormat
        .Min = MIN_VAL
        .Max = MAX_VAL
    End With
End Sub
```

Notice if you use the shape object on a form control, the only way you can change properties of a form control is through the ControlFormat object. Alternatively, you can also use the shorthand naming syntax shown in Listing 5-2.

Listing 5-2. The SetScrollBarLimits Procedure Using the Shorthand Syntax

```
Public Sub SetScrollbarLimits()

    Const MAX_VAL = 20
    Const MIN_VAL = 3
    Dim scrollbr1 As ScrollBar

    Set scrollbr1 = [Scroll Bar 1]

    With scrollbr1
        .Min = MIN_VAL
        .Max = MAX_VAL
    End With
End Sub
```

Often, I'll use the latter method as it is more easily read and intuitively understood. However, you'll notice when you type the As portion of creating your form control object, Scroll Bar won't appear on the list. This can become confusing as usually figuring out the correct object requires guessing at the name (e.g. typing "label", "checkbox", and "scroll bar" to see if they take). So I present both options for you to decide. Throughout the book, I'll prefer the one that to me appears easier to read in context.

The Spinner Control

The Spinner control is fairly similar to the form control Scroll Bar sans the draggable paddle and scroll region between the paddles (see Figure 5-15).

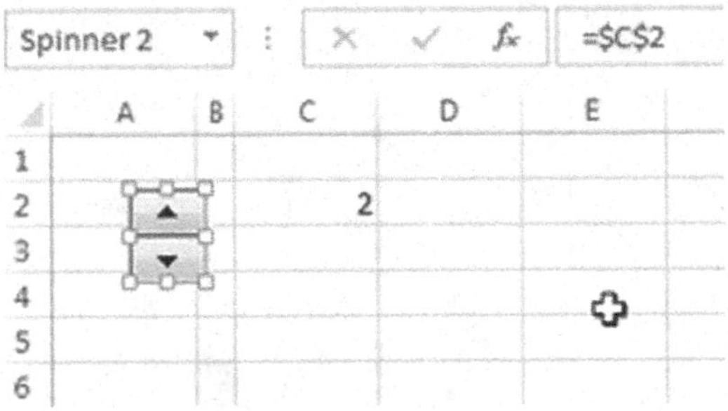

Figure 5-15. An example Spinner control on a spreadsheet

The Spinner control is a useful replacement for a scroll bar in a pinch. However, while the scroll bar can appear both horizontally and vertically on a sheet (see Figure 5-1), the spinner can only appear vertically, as shown in Figure 5-15. You can of course make the spinner larger (and wider, if you'd like), but those up and down paddles will always point in the same direction.

The CheckBox Control

The CheckBox control appears in the first example and it's incredibly versatile. Like the Scroll Bar, the CheckBox control links to cell whose value you can use. Unlike the Scroll Bar, the CheckBox can only take on one of three values (see Figure 5-16). The first two values you should know by heart: TRUE and FALSE. Respectively, they generate a Checked or Unchecked value in the CheckBox.

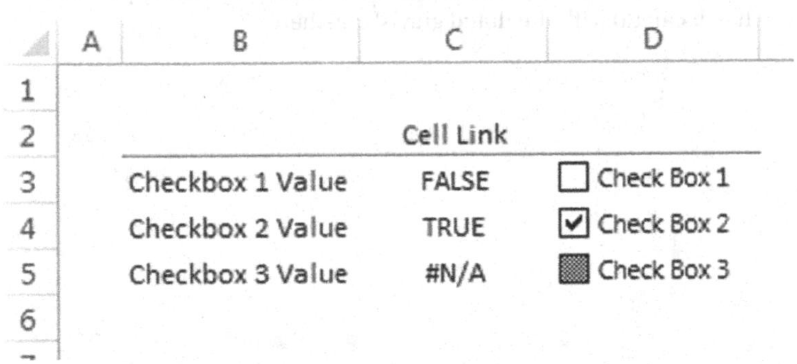

Figure 5-16. A demonstration of the three states possible with a CheckBox

However, check boxes can also take on a fuzzy-gray status called a "mixed" state. The mixed state cannot be set directly by toggling a CheckBox, at least not without some VBA. You can set the mixed state manually by using the =NA() formula in the CheckBox's cell link or by going into its properties dialog box and selecting the Mixed option (see Figure 5-17). You won't use the mixed state in this book, so for now let's focus on the TRUE and FALSE dynamic of the CheckBox.

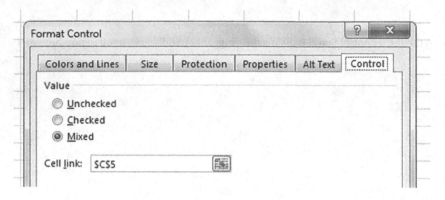

Figure 5-17. The Format Control dialog box for a CheckBox

The Least Favorites: Button, Label, Option Button, and GroupBox Controls

Four controls are left:

- Button

- Label

- Option Button

- GroupBox

In this section I'll provide a little information on why I don't care much for these form controls.

The Button Control

I don't believe you should use the Button control because there are better alternatives. Let's start by taking a look at the Button control in Figure 5-18. There's not much you can do with the dated grayish aesthetic.

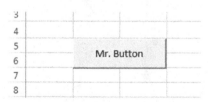

Figure 5-18. A form control Button

An alternative I would suggest is to use an autoshape text box instead. You can still add interactivity to the shape the same way you would with a form control Button by assigning a macro to the shape. The text box will give you much more flexibility in terms of changing its look. In addition, there is no inherent advantage to using the form control Button that is lost when going with an Excel shape.

The Label Control

The Label control is also similarly restrictive. The font size, style, and color of a label cannot be edited directly. Notice in Figure 5-19 that the format buttons have been disabled when the label is selected.

Figure 5-19. *A Label control placed on a spreadsheet*

As a matter of fact, the only way to change a label's style is to link it to a cell with the font styles already set. Take a look at Figure 5-20 to see what I mean. In cell A2, I wrote some text and then set the font color and style in the cell itself. After that, I linked the label directly to the cell. In fact, this is a workaround I discovered accidently; officially, labels aren't supposed to let you change their style. But in any event, a textbox shape does all of this without the hassle.

Figure 5-20. *Even bright and wonderful labels can't overcome certain limitations*

The Option Button Control

Option Button controls are similar to check boxes except that they allow for only one selection. In general, I find they are more trouble than they are worth. ComboBox form controls do essentially the same thing as Option Buttons and take up less screen real estate (see Figure 5-21). For situations where I would like the user to toggle between different states, I like to use text boxes instead (see Figure 5-22). The effect is much cleaner and more visually appealing.

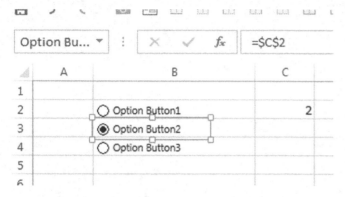

Figure 5-21. *Option butttons laid out and linked to cell C2*

Figure 5-22. *My prefered method for toggling between options*

Figure 5-22 simply shows a group of textboxes with some extra desired formatting. When a user clicks on a textbox, a macro is called to color the textbox a reddish color and the rest a greenish color.

The GroupBox Control

Finally, form GroupBoxes, the last control left undiscussed, are not really useful for anything except grouping components together. They exist purely for aesthetic value. They're not ugly by any stretch, but I'd rather use cell formatting to create a border, especially because it delivers far more options. With the form control GroupBox you only get two options: 3D border or no 3D border. For the sake of an example, Figure 5-23 shows a GroupBox form control over the buttons from Figure 5-22.

Figure 5-23. *The group box surrounds buttons with the group box's border*

Now that you know all the form controls, you'll put the useful ones to good use in a few examples, starting with the Scroll Bar.

Creating Scrollable Tables

Scrollable tables are a great form of Excel form controls. They're easy to implement and often require no VBA, assuming what you want to display isn't complicated (and usually it isn't). At the heart of these tables is the venerable scroll bar. Using the INDEX function and the scroll bar you can create a scrollable region from a larger table of values.

In this example, you will create a scrollable table that pulls data from a larger spreadsheet. The scrollable table will allow you to scroll through a small subset of the data a time. Figure 5-24 shows what the final product will look like. Take a look at Chapter5ScrollableTable.xlsx to grab the data and follow along.

Tornadoes by Year and Month

(1950-1994)

Year	Total	Jan	Feb	Mar	Apr	May	June	July	Aug	Sept	Oct	Nov	Dec
1954	550	2	17	62	113	101	107	45	49	21	14	2	17
1955	593	3	4	43	99	148	153	49	33	15	23	20	3
1956	504	2	47	31	85	79	65	92	42	16	29	7	9
1957	858	17	5	38	216	228	147	55	20	17	18	59	38
1958	564	11	20	15	76	68	128	121	46	24	9	45	1
1959	604	16	20	43	30	226	73	63	38	58	24	11	2
1960	616	9	28	28	70	201	125	42	48	21	18	25	1
1961	697	1	31	124	74	137	107	77	27	53	14	36	16
1962	657	12	25	37	41	200	171	78	51	24	11	5	2
1963	463	15	6	48	84	71	90	62	26	33	13	15	0
Avg	760	13	21	51	102	163	160	88	58	37	23	28	17

Figure 5-24. The final product of your scrollable table

1. To start, insert a new scroll bar into the empty spreadsheet tab in the example file. After that, you must assign a scroll bar to a cell that will hold it. In this example, assign it to A4. This is shown in Figure 5-25.

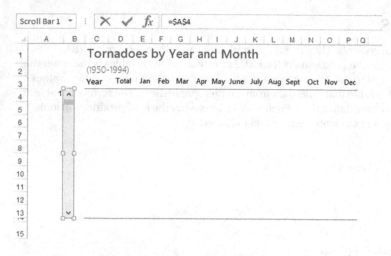

Figure 5-25. *Assiging the scroll bar to a cell value*

2. When creating a scrollable table, you'll have to decide its dimensions. In Figure 5-24, you can see ten items at a time. You'll need to set up a series of dynamic indices, so in A4, write the formula =A3+1 and drag down. Figure 5-26 shows this result and the formulas.

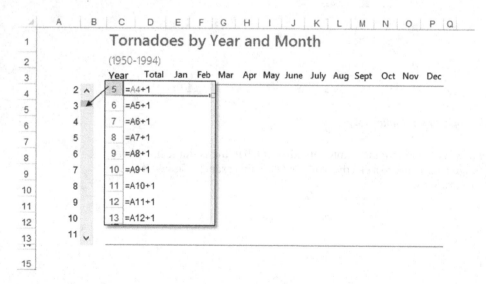

Figure 5-26. *This dynamic will increase all the numbers in the list as changes to the scroll bar are made*

■ **Tip** To help size the scroll bar, use the Snap to Grid feature. Choose a column where you want to house the scroll bar and size the column to the width you'd like the scroll bar to be. Next, after you insert the scroll bar, go to the Format tab and select Snap to Grid from the Align dropdown in the Arrange group. Now resize the scroll bar; you'll see it easily fits to the column.

If you try the scroll bar now, you'll see the dynamic indices increase and decrease with each change in the scroll bar.

3. The backend data for this exercise is on the Data tab. The series of years is named TornadoData.Year, the series of tornado totals is named TornadoData.Totals, and the data range is named TornadoData.DataRegion. By naming these regions you can more easily access them with the INDEX function.

Specifically, you can pull the first row of the data region by using the formula INDEX(TornadoData.DataRegion, $A4,). By leaving that last parameter blank, you can drag the formula across to the desired range and then press Ctrl+Shift+Enter (see Figure 5-27). The last parameter, which takes a column index argument, isn't necessary in this case. By telling Excel that you are using an array formula, Excel knows that the first cell in the region returns the first column index, the second returns the second column index, and so forth. However, for this to work, you must leave that final parameter blank. INDEX(TornadoData.DataRegion, $A4,) is not the same as INDEX(TornadoData.DataRegion, $A4).

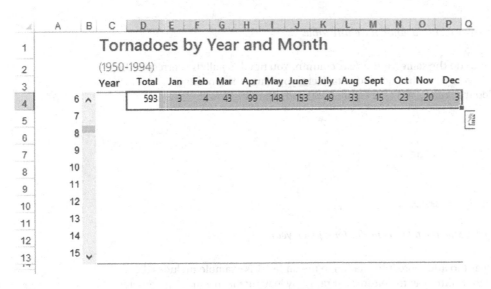

Figure 5-27. *The result of using the Array formula to pull back data*

4. Once you have the first row, you can simply drag down to fill the entire region, as shown in Figure 5-28.

Tornadoes by Year and Month

(1950-1994)

Year	Total	Jan	Feb	Mar	Apr	May	June	July	Aug	Sept	Oct	Nov	Dec
6	593	3	4	43	99	148	153	49	33	15	23	20	3
7	504	2	47	31	85	79	65	92	42	16	29	7	9
8	858	17	5	38	216	228	147	55	20	17	18	59	38
9	564	11	20	15	76	68	128	121	46	24	9	45	1
10	604	16	20	43	30	226	73	63	38	58	24	11	2
11	616	9	28	28	70	201	125	42	48	21	18	25	1
12	697	1	31	124	74	137	107	77	27	53	14	36	16
13	657	12	25	37	41	200	171	78	51	24	11	5	2
14	463	15	6	48	84	71	90	62	26	33	13	15	0
15	704	14	2	36	157	134	137	63	79	25	22	17	18

Figure 5-28. *Dragging the array formula down the entire table*

5. You'll also need to do the same for the Year column. You need to pull the corresponding cell for the given year from the backend data. Here, you'll use the formula INDEX(TornadoData.Year, A4) (see Figure 5-29) and then drag down.

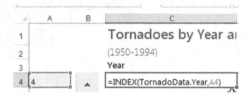

Figure 5-29. *Use INDEX to retrieve the total tornados for a given year*

6. Finally, you'll want to add more information to the table. This example includes the averages for each month over the entire year range by leaving the row index parameter of the INDEX function blank and using a static reference for the column index. This mechanism is similar to what you did above except you are pulling the entire column instead of the entire row. In addition, you are not interested in return each cell in the column; instead, you supply the entire column to an AVERAGE function to get the average for that year (see Figure 5-30).

| | fx | =AVERAGE(INDEX(TornadoData.DataRegion,,E16)) |

	E	F	G	H	I	J	K	L	M	N	O	P	Q
57	12	25	37	41	200	171	78	51	24	11	5	2	
60		21	51	102	163	160	88	58	37	23	28	17	
E16))													
1	2	3	4	5	6	7	8	9	10	11	12		

Figure 5-30. *Use the AVERAGE and INDEX functions to report the average tornados for each month*

7. So that the dynamic indices on the left and the static reference on the bottom do not appear in the table, change those cells to a white font, which blends in with the white background.

8. Finally, set the Minimum Value and Maximum Value fields of the scroll bar (see Figure 5-31).

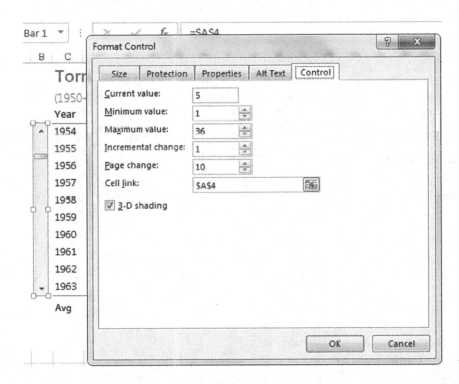

Figure 5-31. *The Format Control dialog box*

The minimum, of course, is 1. The maximum is 36. Why 36? Well, the entire year range is made up of 45 years. That's the last year in the set, 1994, minus the beginning year, 1950. (Remember, you're including 1950 in the set so it comes out to 45 years and not 44.) You show ten years in your table, and you effectively do this by adding nine years to the initial value given by the scrollbar (see Figure 5-32). So the maximum is 45 years minus 9 years, which is 36.

Year
1954
1955
1956
1957
1958
1959
1960
1961
1962
1963

Figure 5-32. *Notice that 1963 equals 1954 plus 9*

Figure 5-33 shows the final table.

Tornadoes by Year and Month

(1950-1994)

Year	Total	Jan	Feb	Mar	Apr	May	June	July	Aug	Sept	Oct	Nov	Dec
1954	550	2	17	62	113	101	107	45	49	21	14	2	17
1955	593	3	4	43	99	148	153	49	33	15	23	20	3
1956	504	2	47	31	85	79	65	92	42	16	29	7	9
1957	858	17	5	38	216	228	147	55	20	17	18	59	38
1958	564	11	20	15	76	68	128	121	46	24	9	45	1
1959	604	16	20	43	30	226	73	63	38	58	24	11	2
1960	616	9	28	28	70	201	125	42	48	21	18	25	1
1961	697	1	31	124	74	137	107	77	27	53	14	36	16
1962	657	12	25	37	41	200	171	78	51	24	11	5	2
1963	463	15	6	48	84	71	90	62	26	33	13	15	0
Avg	760	13	21	51	102	163	160	88	58	37	23	28	17

Figure 5-33. *The final table*

Highlighting Data Points on Charts

You can also use form control scrollbars to highlight a point on a chart. Figure 5-34 shows a time series of the yearly totals of tornados. Below the chart is a scroll bar that moves the black selector point left and right. As the point changes, the label changes with it.

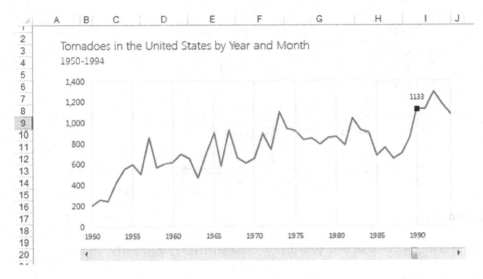

Figure 5-34. *You can highlight data points on the chart using a form control Scroll Bar*

The setup for this problem is somewhat similar to the last. You can follow along in the example file Chapter5DataPoint.xlsx.

First, you start with a scroll bar. This time, however, you draw it horizontally instead of vertically. Again, for precision, it's a good idea to use the Snap to Grid feature. Above, you'll see that columns that border the chart, B and C, are a bit smaller than the rest. I sized these columns about the size of the scroll bar's paddles. That way, the paddle in the scroll area lines up nicely with the selector on the chart. In addition, I was able to nicely align the plot and chart area again using the handy Snap to Grid feature.

The scroll bar is linked to a value on the side of the Excel spreadsheet. The name of the cell is Scrollbar.Value (gee, how creative…). Using the scroll bar's value, you pull the X and Y values using the scroll bar as an index (see Figure 5-35).

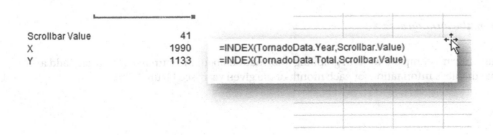

Figure 5-35. *As the scroll bar changes, the X and Y values also change*

Now, this is where the magic happens. You're using a simple scatterplot chart for your timeseries display. Because of this, you don't have to add a huge series to your chart to show the selector. You only need to add the coordinates defined in Figure 5-36. In your chart, you have a series simply named selector that points to the coordinates off to the side. Remember, those coordinates are traced to the value given by the scroll bar. So, as the scroll bar changes, the coordinates update with each change. That's how I came up with the nifty effect.

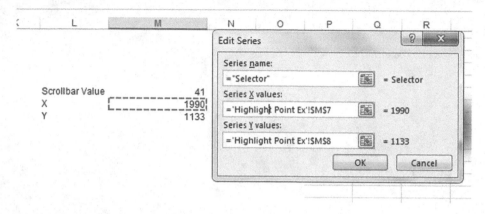

Figure 5-36. *The Edit Series dialog box*

The other series on the chart is simply the totals from your data worksheet tab (see Figure 5-37).

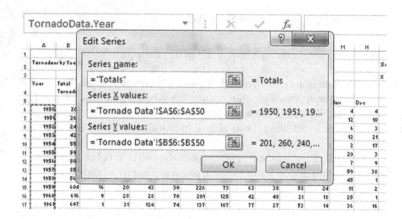

Figure 5-37. *The totals from the tornado data*

But wait! This mechanism isn't complete without grabbing information about the current year. So, let's add a small chart on the side that displays information for each month of the given year (see Figure 5-38).

· and Month

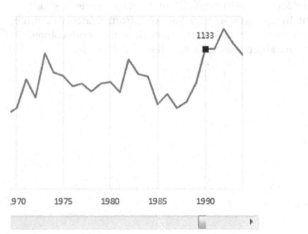

	1990
Jan	11
Feb	57
Mar	86
Apr	108
May	243
Jun	329
Jul	106
Aug	60
Sep	45
Oct	35
Nov	18
Dec	35

***Figure 5-38.** An additional chart displays information for each month of the selected year*

This mechanism is not different from when you looked up rows in the table before. The difference now is that you want to flip that row into a column. So you'll wrap it in the TRANSPOSE function as shown in Figure 5-39. Once you've dragged that function down, you can press Ctrl+Shift+Enter because you're directing Excel to return a range.

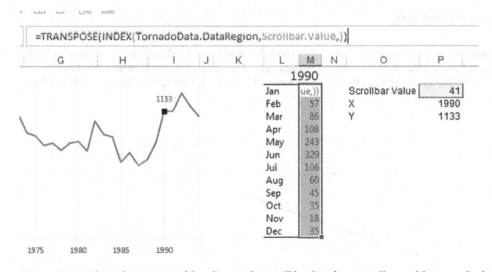

***Figure 5-39.** The information table relies on the scroll bar's value to pull monthly tornado data for a selected year*

The Dynamic Legend

To make a dynamic legend, you use the CheckBox form control for a series in the chart. In this case, however, you won't use the legend Excel provides for you as a chart element. Instead, you'll create your own from scratch! Add three check boxes (clear out the default labels). In addition, write a "minus" sign and add the label next to it, both colored manually. You can see this for yourself by looking at `Chapter5DynamicLegend.xlsx` with the downloads for this chapter.

Figure 5-40 shows that the legend is simply a cell.

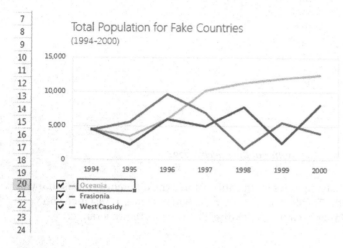

Figure 5-40. *The legends here are simply cells*

Here's how this mechanism works: there are essentially two tables that hold the data presented in this graph. The first table is simply static; you can think of it as a type of database. The second table is an intermediary between the database and chart. You can think of the chart as being the presentation layer. The dynamic is laid out in Figure 5-41.

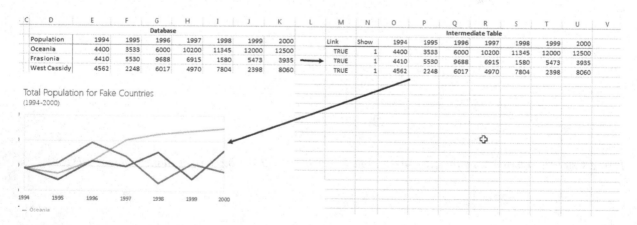

Figure 5-41. *The mechanism of a dynamic legend*

Let's take a closer look at the intermediate table. The first column of the table holds the linked cells of the three check boxes (see Figure 5-42).

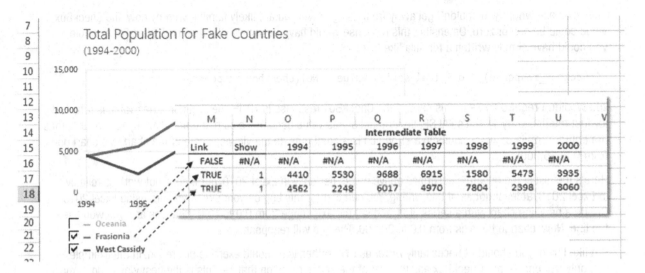

Figure 5-42. *A closer look at the intermediate table*

The next column tests whether the link has returned a TRUE or FALSE. If it returns a TRUE, Excel returns a 1; if it's a FALSE, Excel returns an NA() (see Figure 5-43).

Link	Show		199.
FALSE	=IF(M3,1,NA())		/A
TRUE		1	441(
TRUE		1	456;

Figure 5-43. *If a CheckBox is deselected, you want to return an N/A error*

The cool thing about using NA() is that it returns an #N/A error, which Excel won't plot. In addition to that, anytime you multiply something by an #N/A, it also becomes an #N/A. And that's exactly what you take advantage of in your dynamic legend. The values in the intermediate table are the product of the result of the IF function multiplied by the original values. Figure 5-44 demonstrates this mechanism.

| | | | | fx | =$N3*F3 | | | | | | | | | | | | | | |

C	D	E	F	G	H	I	J	K	L	M	N	O	P	Q	R	S	T	U
					Database										Intermediate Table			
	Population	1994	1995	1996	1997	1998	1999	2000		Link	Show		1994	1995	1996	1997	1998	1999	2000
	Oceania	4400	3533	6000	10200	11345	12000	12500		FALSE	#N/A	#N/A	=$N3*F3	#N/A	#N/A	#N/A	#N/A	#N/A
	Frasionia	4410	5530	9688	6915	1580	5473	3935		TRUE	1		4410	5530	9688	6915	1580	5473	3935

Figure 5-44. *The dynamic legend works by turning the values in a series into an #N/A error and thus removing it from the chart*

WAIT…WHY AM I USING IF()? I THOUGHT YOU SAID I SHOULDN'T USE IT?

This is a case where you couldn't get away from using IF. As you are likely familiar with by now, the CheckBox's value could be one or zero. Ostensibly, this response would have been perfect as the multiplier. For example, you could have simply written a formula like this:

```
=(checkbox_response) * original_series_value - NOT(checkbox_response)
```

You wouldn't require an IF in this case. If the CheckBox response is TRUE, the original series value is returned (or just multiplied by 1). If it's FALSE, the original series value becomes a zero and NOT(FALSE) returns a 1; thus, the entire formula of =0-1 results in a -1, which is a point outside the viewing scale of the chart (the chart goes from 0 to 15,000).

Here's the issue: the dynamic described above works perfectly in Excel 2010, but it does not work as reliably in Excel 2013, at least not as of this writing. You can test for this bug on your own if you are using Excel 2013. Create a new line chart with a series of -1 and set the axis range from 0.0 to 10.0. Chances are, you won't see the line. Now, change the axis from 0.0 to 20,000. The line will reappear.

But like I said, you shouldn't necessarily *never* use IF; rather, you should exercise discretion. In the example, you only use one IF per CheckBox and the rest of the series relies on that IF. This is the best way to do it. You could have alternatively made each datapoint in the intermediate table also be a test against the response of the CheckBox. That would have employed far too many IF statements than necessary.

The Last Word

In this chapter, you learned how truly awesome form controls are. They're flexible, don't often require much code, and can be moved and placed rather easily. As you can probably guess, you'll return to form controls several times through the rest of the book.

PART II

■ ■ ■

A Real World Example

In this part, you examine and investigate a real world example based on many of the core concepts introduced in the first part. This real-world example is inspired by a real spreadsheet I developed for a client.

Chapter 6 proposes a new method of taking in user input by using the spreadsheet rather than ActiveX controls and UserForms. You begin by investigating a very simple Excel-based input form and learn how custom formats can aid in form validation. You then move onto a more complicated example of user input—a spreadsheet-based wizard. You spend the rest of the chapter reverse engineering the components of the wizard and learning the mechanics.

Chapter 7 takes you through a type of storage pattern using the spreadsheet as the database while also extending the wizard built in the previous chapter. You'll reverse engineer several of the spreadsheet components. Throughout the chapter, I'll show you how to add, delete, and edit records with methods that are based on both formulas and code.

Chapter 8 will implement a real world model built on top of the wizard from the previous chapters. You begin by reviewing metrics from a real study by the World Health Organization and implement a weighted average model based on the study. You then develop features of the analysis portion of your model to allow for sorting and scrolling using form controls.

Chapter 9 focuses on perfecting the presentation of the spreadsheet application you've built over the previous three chapters. You work on implementing a one-way sensitivity analysis system for the metric weights. You also incorporate a formula-based sorting method. Finally, you review design aesthetics and decide upon the best colors and layout to use so as not to overwhelm the visual field.

CHAPTER 6

■ ■ ■

Getting Input from Users

This chapter begins the second half of the book. From this chapter and on, you'll be creating a spreadsheet-based application using many of the principles discussed in the first few chapters. To get an idea of what you're building, you can download the completed version, Chapter9Final.xlsm, from within this book's project files.

From this point forward, you might also notice a change in the learning format. Many books will have you build your components from scratch. You did just this in previous chapters of the book. However, going forward, I will present you with completed work whose functions you'll reverse engineer. In that way, you're going to apply the principles from the previous chapters (as well as learn a few more along the way).

There are two good reasons for this teaching style. First, in the real world, you won't always start from scratch. Sometimes you'll receive work built by someone else. You have to reverse engineer what they've completed and also add your own features. Many of the examples files going forward are much like that inherited spreadsheet. You should know how they work, but I also want you to think creatively of how they can be extended (and tailored) for your use.

The second reason goes back to the phrase mentioned in a previous chapter—that of reusable components. Many of the features I'll describe are not steps in a larger spreadsheet. Rather, they exist in their own right. They're as applicable here as they are for other spreadsheet projects. Recall from the first chapter I said the most important skill to succeed in this book is creativity. That creativity will help you understand how to implement these components in your work.

The bulk of this chapter deals with creating a spreadsheet-based input wizard with Excel. But before diving into the wizard, I'll discuss creating simple spreadsheet-based forms and why they're often the better choice compared to UserForms. From there, you'll start with a completed version of the spreadsheet-based wizard. I'll walk you through several of the design components, including proper layout, input pages, and features of the user interface. By the end of the chapter, you should see how building a spreadsheet-based input wizard is consistent with building faster and leaner Excel applications.

■ **Note**   You can download project files for this chapter along with the other example files for this book from the Source Code/Downloads tab at www.apress.com /9781484207352.

Of Input Forms and Excel

Most Excel developers would prefer UserForms to capture user input, especially when the user input has multiple steps. Indeed, conventional wisdom often argues for using UserForms and ActiveX controls. The problem is that ActiveX controls can be somewhat finicky and unpredictable, as established in Chapter 5. Remember this figure from Chapter 5 (Figure 6-1)?

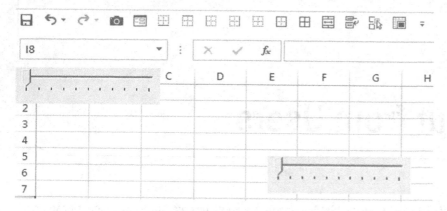

Figure 6-1. *This is the same ActiveX control shown in two different locations*

UserForms are a type of ActiveX control and they suffer from the same unpredictability. For instance, UserForms will sometimes appear different across different computers. This is the result of different internal settings and hardware. Monitor resolution, DPI, and Windows' internal font default can potentially cause these unwanted effects.

One way to get around all of this is develop input forms directly on the spreadsheet. This is what I advocate. It may seem like a hard task at first, but you will soon find it provides flexibility not found when using UserForms. In addition, the spreadsheet provides a better canvas upon which to create a more aesthetically pleasing experience. The dull grey scheme that appears by default in the UserForms feels almost anachronistic in this day and age, a relic of a bygone era. Figure 6-2 shows an example UserForm I pulled from Microsoft's Developer Network's help pages.

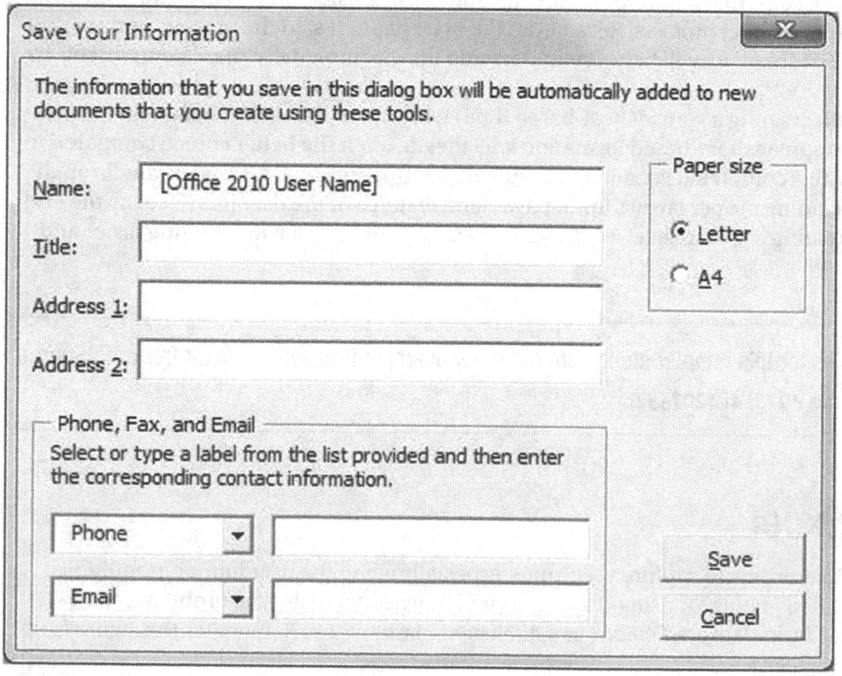

Figure 6-2. *An example of a UserForm found in Microsoft's Excel help*

Let's take a look at what you can do when you create input forms on the spreadsheet instead.

A Simple Input Form

In this section, I'll discuss how to create a simple input form. Open `Chapter6SimpleInput.xlsx` to follow along. Figure 6-3 is a snapshot of the input form in `Chapter6SimpleInput.xlsx`.

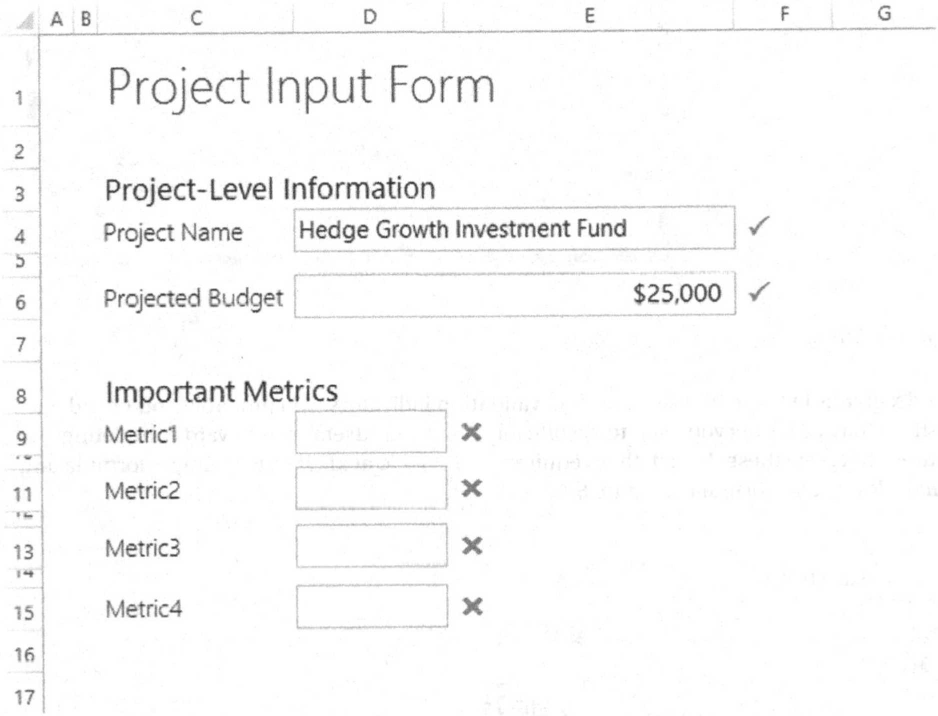

Figure 6-3. *A spreadsheet-based input form*

You can create a new input form in Excel with nothing more than an unused worksheet tab. With an idea of the information you'd like to collect at hand, it's a simple matter of laying everything out.

Nothing too fancy goes into creating something like this. Each input box is simply a named range. If you've ever created an input form on UserForm before, you know that each input TextBox is given a name. For instance, convention would tell us the name for TextBox on a UserForm that stores a Project Name would go by txtProjectName. You're doing a similar action by name each cell with a named range. The named range, as you shall see, will give you easy programmatic access to the cell's value later on down the road. Figure 6-4 shows the named ranges and the input cells they point to.

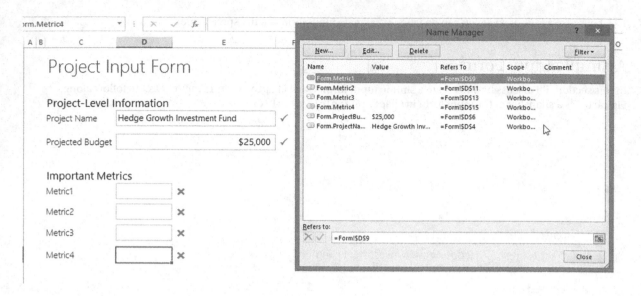

Figure 6-4. *Input items are named ranges*

The green checks and red x glyphs in Figure 6-4 serve as data validation indicators. You probably don't need one for each and every box, but there may be inputs you want to specifically point your users' eyes toward completing. There's no fancy coding required to create these. In fact, they require no VBA code at all. It's just a simple formula and some custom formatting. Take a look at the formula in Figure 6-5.

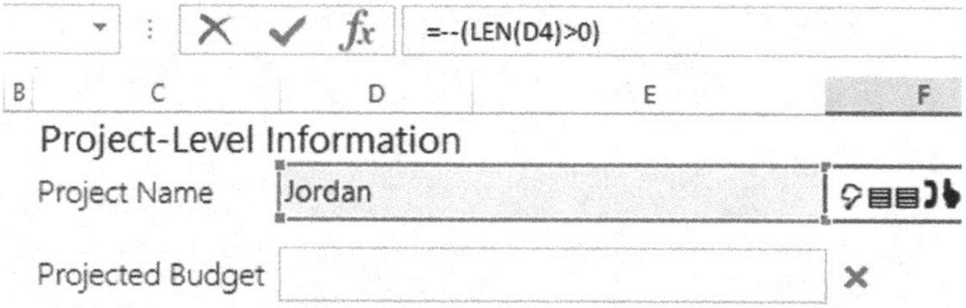

Figure 6-5. *A visual validation formula you can use for input*

Here, you're simply testing whether the length of the text entered in the adjacent cell is greater than zero. If it is, that means something has been written in the cell. If the length of text is zero, that means no input has been provided. Recall that the double-dash is shorthand for converting the Boolean values of TRUE and FALSE into zero and one.

If you take a closer look at Figure 6-5, you'll notice that the formula in the cell is not readable text. The reason is because to get the checkbox and x symbols, I used the Wingdings 2 font.

Custom Formats for Input Validation

In this section, I'll talk about how custom formats can help turn those zeros and ones into x's and checkmarks. It's simple; you use custom formatting. In Figure 6-6, I've used the custom formatting syntax to tell Excel what to display when the number is either a one or zero.

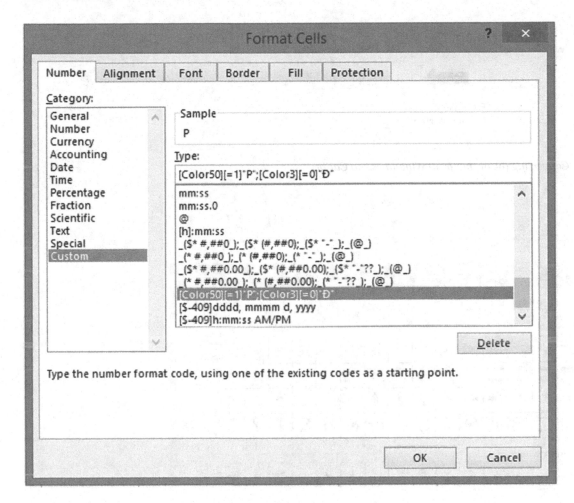

Figure 6-6. *Custom formats are shown in the Format Cells dialog box*

So let's break this down. With custom formats, I can create conditions to let Excel know when to display which symbol. For example, I have two conditions in the above formula. Can you guess what they look like? If you notice [=1] and [=0] then you're spot on! These blocks of syntax outline are the conditions. Note that the semicolon separates each condition.

Now take a look at the two character symbols that are being returned. There's a "P" and a really weird looking "Đ" thing. To get these characters, I actually looked them up using the Symbol dialog box from on the Insert tab (see Figure 6-8). In this case, I selected Wingdings 2 as the font and inserted into Excel the symbols I desired. When Excel inserts these symbols into the worksheet, they'll be in the Wingdings 2 font.

But if you look again at Figure 6-6, you'll see the input box in the Format Cells dialog box is looking for regular alphanumeric characters—not symbols. So you'll need to get those Windings 2 symbols back into regular text. The easiest way to do this is to select the cell in which you've inserted the symbol and change it to a normal font, like Arial, Calibri, or Times New Roman. Figure 6-7 demonstrates what happens when you convert the output from Wingdings 2 to Calibri.

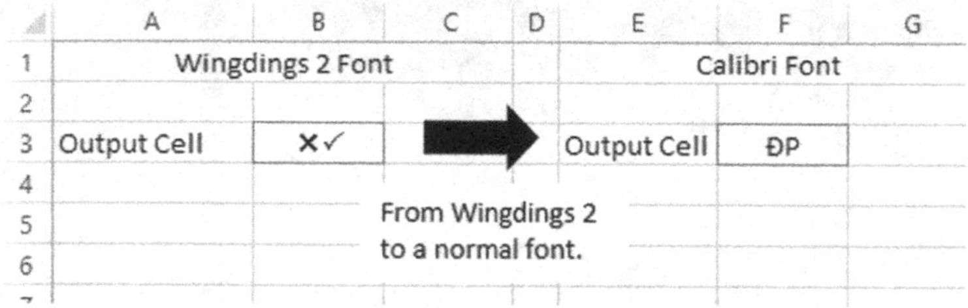

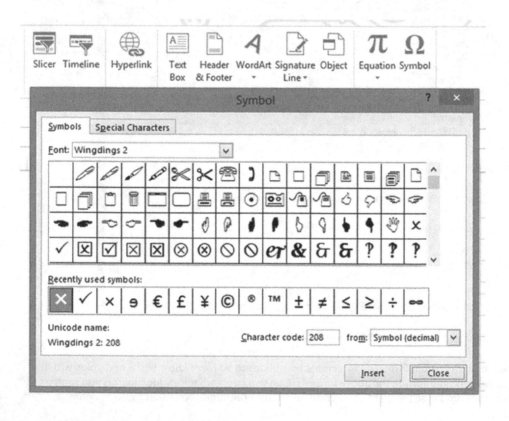

Figure 6-7. *Converting the output from Wingdings 2 to Calibri*

Figure 6-8. *The Insert Symbol dialog box*

Finally, you'll notice the other two syntax blocks in Figure 6-6 that look like [ColorXX], where XX is some number. The XX in this case is in fact a number that points to a specific color index. To see a full list of colors to choose from, go to http://dmcritchie.mvps.org/excel/colors.htm.

The basic syntax for custom formats used here is [Color XX][condition]<symbol to return>. There are other format options available, and I encourage you to take a look at them. But they are beyond the scope of this book.

Based on what you've learned so far, you're now ready to begin building a spreadsheet wizard to take input from the user. Notice that this simple input form can be created rather quickly and uses only formulas. The same form would take longer to create if made on a UserForm.

Creating a Spreadsheet-Based Wizard

In this section, you'll build off the input form created from the previous section. However, you'll also spend considerable time on the layout mechanics of a spreadsheet-based wizard. As stated in the beginning of the chapter, you'll focus on components rather than building from scratch. I recommend following along by opening Chapter6Wizard.xlsm from within the project files.

In Figure 6-9, you can see the beginnings of a spreadsheet-based wizard that will serve as the backbone for the spreadsheet application you complete in forthcoming chapters. If you have Chapter6Wizard.xlsm open, I recommend going through all the interactive components.

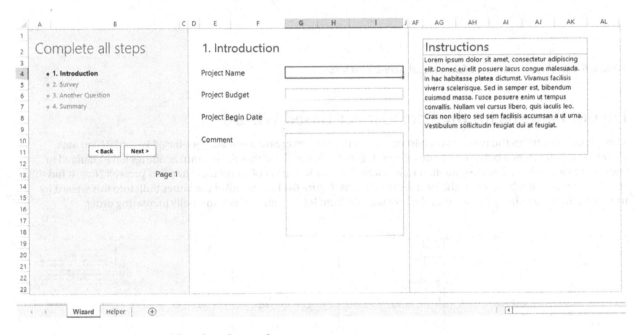

Figure 6-9. *A beautiful spreadsheet-based wizard*

For instance, a user can use the back and next buttons (Figure 6-9) and the current page in the middle will change to reflect the choice. Figure 6-9 shows the Introduction page of the wizard.

Figure 6-10 shows the screen for the second page after pressing the Next button on the first page.

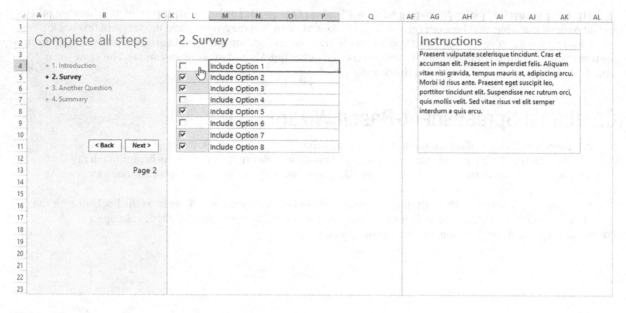

Figure 6-10. *Page 2, Survey, of the spreadsheet-based wizard*

Layout Patterns for the Spreadsheet-Based Wizard

This section discusses the proper spreadsheet layout required to create a spreadsheet-based wizard. If you look closely at the difference between Figure 6-9 and Figure 6-10, you'll see that the column headings have changed in the center view. This is because the first view referred to a different set of columns. When you pressed Next, it hid this set of columns and advanced to the next set of columns. Figure 6-11 shows all of the panes built into this wizard by unhiding the entire sheet. Notice that they are laid out from left to right an incrementally increasing order.

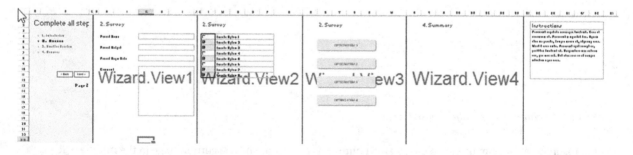

Figure 6-11. *A view of the spreadsheet-based wizard with every item unhidden*

The mechanism shows and hides these columns accordingly. If you unhide everything and then zoom out, you can see each of these views laid out accordingly.

Note that I've named these views successively: View1, View2, View3, etc. In this setup, it makes it easy to know which view you are currently on. As well, you can know the successive panes in the list in either direction, whether you go forward or backward. Consider, if you were on View2, you'd know the previous screen would be View1 and the next screen would be View3.

Think about the ease of this setup. If you want to make changes to each step, you simple need to make them in that step's set of columns. If you'd like to add another step, you could insert another series of columns in front of Wizard.View4 and name it Wizard.View5. The Name Manager can help you keep track of how many views you have (see Figure 6-12). In addition, you can jump to the step you want automatically by selecting its name.

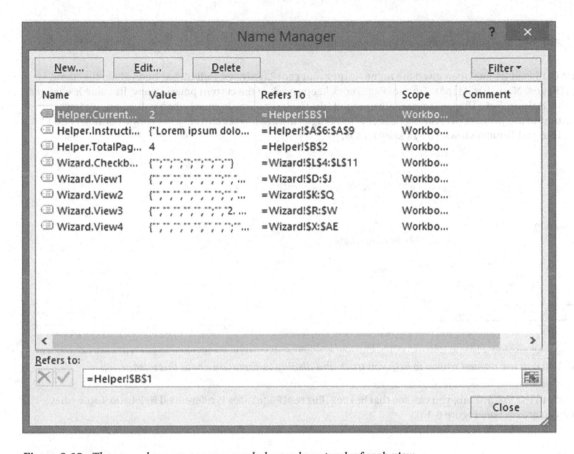

Figure 6-12. *The named range manager can help you keep track of each view*

The Helper Tab

In this section I'll talk about the Helper tab (see Figure 6-13), which is an integral part of the spreadsheet-based wizard.

Figure 6-13. *The Helper tab keeps track of important information for the wizard*

As has been the case with previous spreadsheets, I always suggest placing extra information either in a hidden spot on the spreadsheet or in another tab. In this case, you have several items in the Helper tab (see Figure 6-14).

	A	B	C	D	E
1	Current Page Index	1	<--Helper.CurrentPageIndex		
2	Total Pages	4	<-- Helper.TotalPages		
3					

Figure 6-14. *A snapshot of named ranges on the Helper tab*

In Figure 6-15, cell B1 has been given the name Helper.CurrentPageIndex. Cell B2 has been given the name Helper.TotalPages. Note that Helper.CurrentPageIndex keeps track of the current page in view. Its value is changed within the code. Helper.TotalPages is manually updated (that is, by you, the human) when you add new views. You could automate the process of ensuring Helper.TotalPages always has the correct total views. For now, I don't foresee you adding additional views, so let's keep it as is.

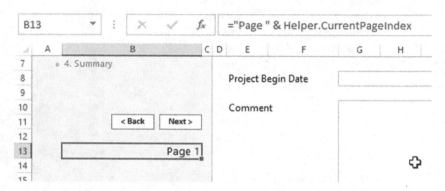

Figure 6-15. *You can use named ranges to help you track and display information about this wizard*

Going back to the Wizard tab, you can see that Helper.CurrentPageIndex is referenced to let you know what page number you are on (see Figure 6-15).

Moving Between Views

For your wizard to have its full effect, you need a way to move back and forth between the views. That's what the Next and Back buttons on the wizard help you do. The following code listings show the code that is called when you press forward (Listing 6-1) and backward (Listing 6-2).

Listing 6-1. This Code Will Tell the Wizard to Display the Next View

```
Public Sub GoNext()
    Dim index As Integer

    ' Read in the current page index and increment it by one
    ' to go next
    index = [Helper.CurrentPageIndex]
    index = index + 1

    ' Check if we're already on the last page
    If index > [Helper.TotalPages] Then Exit Sub
```

```
        ' Unhide the next view
        Wizard.Range("Wizard.View" & index).Columns.Hidden = False

        ' Check to see if we're on a page that requires special instructions
        If index = 2 Then
            DisplayCheckboxes
        Else
            HideCheckboxes
        End If

        ' Hide the current set of columns
        If index > 1 Then
            Wizard.Range("Wizard.View" & index - 1).Columns.Hidden = True
        End If

        'Set Helper.CurrentPageIndex equal to the next page index
        [Helper.CurrentPageIndex] = index
End Sub
```

Listing 6-2. This Code Will Tell the Wizard to Display the Previous View

```
Public Sub GoPrevious()
    Dim index As Integer

        ' Read in the current page index and decrement it by one
        ' to go previous
        index = [Helper.CurrentPageIndex]
        index = index - 1

        ' Check if we're already on the first page
        If index < 1 Then Exit Sub

        ' Unhide the previous view
        Wizard.Range("Wizard.View" & index).Columns.Hidden = False

        ' Check to see if we're on a page that requires special instructions
        If index = 2 Then
            DisplayCheckboxes
        Else
            HideCheckboxes
        End If

        ' Hide the current set of columns
        If index < [Helper.TotalPages] Then
            Wizard.Range("Wizard.View" & index + 1).Columns.Hidden = True
        End If

        'Set Helper.CurrentPageIndex equal to the previous page index
        [Helper.CurrentPageIndex] = index

End Sub
```

Take a look through both listings. Notice that they are very similar except for a few minor differences. The GoNext procedure checks to see if you've reached the end of the set of views while the GoPrevious procedure checks if you're still at the beginning. The GoNext procedure increments the current page index, while the GoPrevious procedure decrements the current page index. This is another example of a reusable component—the mechanism to go forward and backward is virtually the same, so you just need to make a few accommodations. If you think about creating a general mechanism, then reusing and adjusting the code is easy.

Views That Require Additional Instruction

Some views require extra instruction before they're displayed. For example, Figure 6-16 shows a series of check boxes, which require additional explanation.

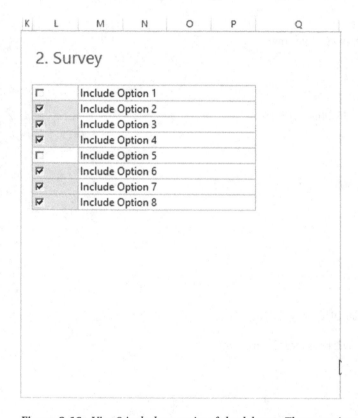

Figure 6-16. *View2 includes a series of check boxes. These require special instructions*

Unlike input cells form on other views, the check boxes are form controls (CheckBox). They sit on top of the spreadsheet. It's not enough to simply hide the form controls by hiding the view on which they reside. The reason is that form controls don't always become hidden so cleanly when you hide a column, even when you set them to move and size with cells in their properties. So you may be wondering how to ensure that these check boxes always appear in the correct location. The answer is a technique I've come up with called *anchoring*.

Anchoring Controls

In this section, I'll talk about how to anchor your controls so they always appear in the same spot when you hide and unhide columns or rows. The first thing you need to do is name your desired controls as part of a series. Let's go back to that second view. Figure 6-17 highlights the first check box in the series.

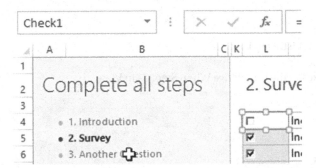

Figure 6-17. *This check box is anchored to the underlying cell*

Notice that the name of the check box is Check1. The check box below it is named Check2, and below that is Check3, all the way through to Check8. Furthermore, in Figure 6-18, I've selected the range that appears under each check box. Notice I've named it Wizard.CheckboxAnchor. This anchor will be your guide in placing these check boxes.

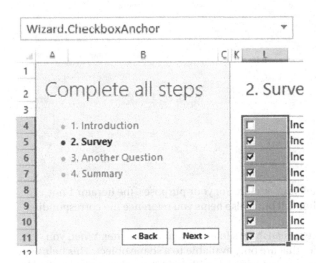

Figure 6-18. *You can create a range of anchors for a set of check boxes*

Now recall this snippet of code from GoNext and GoPrevious, shown in Listing 6-1 and Listing 6-2. When you are showing the second view, View2, you call the procedure DisplayCheckboxes; when you leave the second view, you call the procedure HideCheckboxes. Listing 6-3 excerpts this code.

Listing 6-3. An Excerpt from GoNext

```
' Check to see if we're on a page that requires special instructions
If index = 2 Then
    DisplayCheckboxes
Else
    HideCheckboxes
End If
```

Now let's take a look at the DisplayCheckboxes shown in Listing 6-4.

Listing 6-4. DisplayCheckboxes Will Anchor the Check Boxes to the Cell Range When Step2 Is in View

```
Private Sub DisplayCheckboxes()
    Dim i As Integer

    'Iterate through each cell in our anchor
    For i = 1 To [Wizard.CheckboxAnchor].Rows.Count

        'Create a shape object to point to our current Checkbox
        Dim CurrentCheckbox As Excel.Shape
        Set CurrentCheckbox = Me.Shapes("Check" & i)

        'Set the checkbox to be the exact same size as the
        'as the cell it sits atop
        With [Wizard.CheckboxAnchor].Rows(i).Cells
            CurrentCheckbox.Width = .Width
            CurrentCheckbox.Height = .Height
            CurrentCheckbox.Top = .Top
            CurrentCheckbox.Left = .Left
        End With

        'Ensure people can see it
        CurrentCheckbox.Visible = True
    Next i
End Sub
```

In this code, you iterate through every cell that constitutes your anchor. For your purposes, the iterator i not only helps you track your current location through each anchor cell but it also helps you reference the corresponding check box.

You'll notice that I reference each check box through the spreadsheet's internal shape container. When you treat check boxes as shapes, you are exposed to the properties that are only available to a shape object. This helps because the check box object does not always show its properties and methods with IntelliSense (more on that later in the chapter).

In the line With [Wizard.CheckboxAnchor].Rows(i).Cells, you are grabbing the current cell in your anchor given at index i. With that current cell, you can tell the check box with the same name given by index i—that is, if you are on cell 1 in Wizard.CheckboxAnchor, use the check box with the name Check1. You then tell that check box to be the exact same width and height, and the same top and left. This ensures the check box takes up the entire width of any cell in your anchor. You can see this effect in Figure 6-17.

When you're not on the second view, you'll want to hide these check boxes. Listing 6-5 shows how you do just that.

Listing 6-5. This Code Will Remove the Check Boxes from the Anchored Cells

```
Private Sub HideCheckboxes()

    Dim i As Integer

    'Iterate through each cell in our anchor
    For i = 1 To [Wizard.CheckboxAnchor].Rows.Count

        'Create a shape object to point to our current Checkbox
        Dim CurrentCheckbox As Excel.Shape
        Set CurrentCheckbox = Me.Shapes("Check" & i)

        'Set the checkbox to be the exact same size as the
        'as the cell it sits atop
        With [Wizard.CheckboxAnchor].Rows(i).Cells
            CurrentCheckbox.Top = 0
            CurrentCheckbox.Left = 0
            CurrentCheckbox.Width = 0
            CurrentCheckbox.Height = 0
        End With

        'Ensure the checkbox is no longer visible
        CurrentCheckbox.Visible = False

    Next i
End Sub
```

Just as GoPrevious was similar to GoNext, but in a different direction, HideCheckBoxes is very similar to DisplayCheckboxes. It simply undoes the work performed in DisplayCheckboxes.

But you may be wondering, is it even necessary to change the *height, width, top, and left if you're just going to hide the check boxes?* The truth is, it may not be. You could simply hide these check boxes without doing anything else. At least, at a product level it makes no difference. However, while developing anchors on your spreadsheet, moving every unused check box to a safe location is a good idea.

Here's why. Excel acts somewhat unpredictably when working with form controls. If the above code errors out because there was a bug in the original loop, you might notice the check boxes didn't disappear as they should have. Sometimes, Excel will make several copies of the same CheckBox control (one on top of the other). What causes this is an error in your code while working with multiple form controls. By moving each control to a safe location, you can monitor when Excel has made copies of itself.

Anchoring for Large Sets of Controls

In the previous section's example, one could easily insert eight check boxes and then name them accordingly. It's not necessarily the most enjoyable of exercises, but it's a simple and quick task. What happens if you have so many controls that this take becomes incredibly burdensome? In this section, I'll talk about a quick method of anchoring for large regions.

In Figure 6-19, I've created a large check box anchor region, which I've highlighted in gray for demonstration purposes. Like the anchor region above, I've made this region a named range.

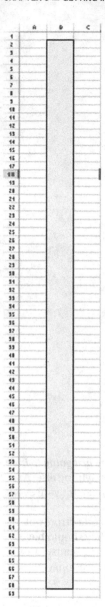

Figure 6-19. *Inserting several check boxes and naming each one for large regions such as this is an onerous task*

You can quickly create enough check boxes for this entire region by reusing elements of the above presented code. Listing 6-6 shows the code you can use to quickly fill up the entire region with check boxes.

Listing 6-6. This Code Will Fill in a Predefined Anchor Region with Check Boxes

```
Public Sub FillCheckboxAnchorRegion()

    'Clear out any checkboxes already created.
    'This will ensure we don't duplicate checkbox
    'names.
    Me.CheckBoxes.Delete

    Dim i As Integer

    For i = 1 To [CheckboxAnchor].Rows.Count

        Dim CurrentCell As Range
        Dim NewCheckbox As CheckBox

        Set CurrentCell = [CheckboxAnchor].Cells(i)
        Set NewCheckbox = Me.CheckBoxes.Add(0, 0, 0, 0)
        With CurrentCell
            NewCheckbox.Width = .Width
            NewCheckbox.Height = .Height
            NewCheckbox.Top = .Top
            NewCheckbox.Left = .Left
        End With

        NewCheckbox.Name = "Check" & i
    Next

End Sub
```

This code is fairly straightforward. Every worksheet contains a collections object that holds all the CheckBox controls that appear on the sheet. Be careful, however; the collection is not immediately available through IntelliSense. So you need to trust that it is there, even if IntelliSense doesn't show it. When the check boxes are already created, sometimes it's easier to refer to them using the Shapes collection as you did earlier in the chapter.

The Checkbox collections object has an Add method. The parameters for this method are left, top, width, and height. Given this, you might be wondering why I would supply this argument with zeros and then adjust the checkbox's dimensions thereafter. However, in my experience, sometimes changing the width and height after setting the CheckBox control's coordinates will slightly change its position. Therefore, your best bet is to set the dimensions first and then set the coordinates.

Finally, you might have noticed in these examples when a check box is selected, its background will change to help you easily visualize which options have been selected at a glance. I'll talk more about how to do that in the next chapter.

In the meantime, let's talk about how to provide information about the page you're on.

Components That Provide Information

This section will describe how to develop components in the spreadsheet-based wizard that provide the user with information. This includes highlighting the steps you're on, describing the page you're looking at, and including page-specific instructions to the user. Figure 6-20 highlights these components.

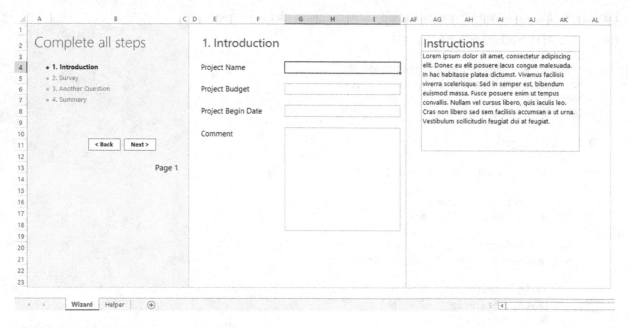

Figure 6-20. *Highlighting components that provide information*

Using Custom Formats to Highlight the Current Step

This section will cover how you can use custom formats (as you did in the first examples in this chapter) to help you highlight which step is currently in view. Figure 6-21 shows an excerpt of the formula. This is essentially the same formula for all the possible steps cells in Column A.

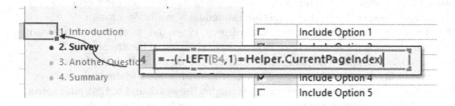

Figure 6-21. *The large formula appears in the selected cell*

Let's break down this formula. Recall that -- is simply the shorthand operation to change a text string or Boolean expression into a number. Because every step starts with a given number (e.g. 1. Introduction, 2. Survey, etc), you can read in that number. In Figure 6-21, we read in that number by looking at the first character of each step. Left(B4, 1) will return a 1; Left(B5, 1) will return a 2 and so forth. You use the shorthand value operation to turn it into a number.

Once you know the number, you can simply use a Boolean conditional to compare it to the current page you're on. In Figure 6-19, --LEFT(B4,1)=Helper.CurrentPageIndex would return a FALSE. This is because you are on the second page, and cell A4 refers to the first page. Cell A5 refers to the second page, so it will return a TRUE. The final -- at the end converts the TRUE and FALSE values back to zeros and ones.

To create the dot effects above, you follow a similar custom formula described in the beginning. To all of them, I've applied this simple custom format syntax: [Color15][=0]●;[Color9][=1]●.

Using INDEX to Provide Step-Specific Information

This section will cover the finishing touches to your wizard. On the top of every view, I've placed the same formula throughout. You can see this formula in Figure 6-22.

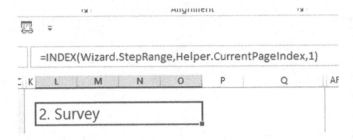

Figure 6-22. *You can use the INDEX formula to display view-specific information*

In Figure 6-23, you can see that `Wizard.StepRange` points to the list of steps on the side.

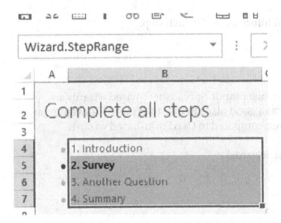

Figure 6-23. *The selected region comprises of the names of all available steps in the wizard*

Because `Wizard.CurrentPageIndex` will always refer to the current step in view, you can simply place this formula at the top of each wizard page. This will ensure you always show the correct heading. In addition, you can simply change the title of the step in `Wizard.StepRange` and the change will be reflected automatically in its corresponding view.

The instructions follows a similar path. There's an Instructions Table on the Helper tab that includes instructions for each step. The Instructions Table holds particular instructions for each page in the wizard. Take a look at the instructions formula used in Figure 6-24.

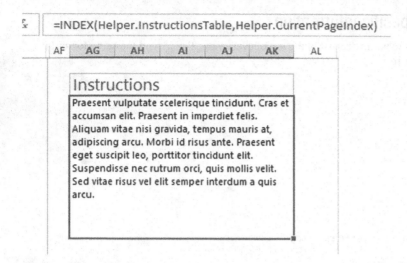

=INDEX(Helper.InstructionsTable,Helper.CurrentPageIndex)

Instructions

Praesent vulputate scelerisque tincidunt. Cras et accumsan elit. Praesent in imperdiet felis. Aliquam vitae nisi gravida, tempus mauris at, adipiscing arcu. Morbi id risus ante. Praesent eget suscipit leo, porttitor tincidunt elit. Suspendisse nec rutrum orci, quis mollis velit. Sed vitae risus vel elit semper interdum a quis arcu.

Figure 6-24. *Similar to the mechanism described in Figure 6-22, you can use INDEX to pull specific instructions*

Again, you use the current page index to help you pull relevant information for each step.

The Last Word

In this chapter, I talked about building spreadsheets that can capture user input. Spreadsheet-based wizards are particularly useful. You may not have thought that a spreadsheet was a good place to take user input. Conventional wisdom suggests that you should use ActiveX components. However, compared to UserForm-based wizards, spreadsheet-based wizards are easier to build, design, and modify.

In the next chapter, I'll talk about how to store input from these wizards.

■ ■ ■

CHAPTER 7

Storage Patterns for User Input

In the last chapter, I discussed developing the components of a spreadsheet-based wizard. The main example from last chapter had you review the infrastructure required to create a spreadsheet-based wizard. Whereas the last chapter concerned layout mechanics of creating an input interface, this chapter will deal with how to store the information once the user has finished their input. What follows builds from the previous chapter. You'll still use the spreadsheet-based wizard implementation described in the previous chapter. However, going forward, you'll make a few changes, which you'll see here soon.

In this chapter, I'll begin by describing a system of metrics that will become the inputs for your wizard. From there, I'll describe the database scheme used to store information once it's been completed. Finally, I'll discuss handling typical database functions, like inserting a new record or deleting an existing one.

The World Health Organization: An Applied Example

In 2000, the World Health Organization ranked the healthcare systems of several different industrialized nations in a study called the *World Health Report 2000 – Health systems: Improving performance*. The study used five key metrics defined here:

- **Health Level**: Measures life expectancy for a given country.

- **Responsiveness**: Measures factors such as speed to health service, access to doctors, et al.

- **Financial Fairness**: Measures the fairness of who shoulders the burden of financial costs in a country.

- **Health Distribution**: Measures the level of equitable distribution of healthcare in a country.

- **Responsiveness Distribution**: Measures the level of equitable distribution of responsiveness defined above.

I'll make some slight modifications to the original model used by the World Health Organization. For one, each country can score from 1 to 10 for a given metric. Second, I've generated a list of made-up countries. So, to be sure, all the data presented herein is notional. Except for the metrics used above (and the weights used in later chapters), the results have basically nothing to do with the actual results of the real model. That's right, all data herein is fictitious. Any resemblance to real life data is purely coincidental. No spreadsheets were harmed in the writing of this book.

In this chapter, you'll allow the user to create a new country, score each country based on metrics, and then store each result into a database. All of this will be self-contained in one spreadsheet file. In addition, you'll be following many of the themes presented in previous chapters. You'll rely heavily on named ranges and attempt to minimize unnecessary use of code.

Design of Your Spreadsheet File

You'll be using the example file `Chapter7Wizard.xlsm` for this chapter. The file is made up of five of tabs, shown in Figure 7-1.

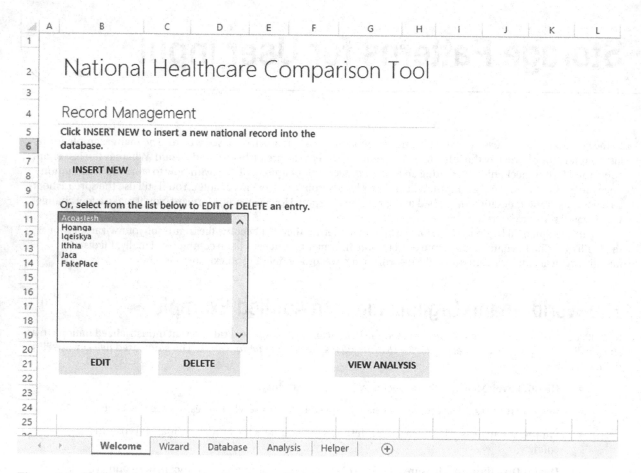

***Figure 7-1.** The five tabs you'll be using for your workbook*

Let's go through each of these tabs.

- **Welcome:** Welcome is essentially your menu. When the user first opens the spreadsheet, it's what they should see (think: "Welcome screen"). Figure 7-2 in the following section shows what the menu looks like.

- **Wizard:** Wizard contains your spreadsheet-based wizard.

- **Database:** Database contains the backend database you'll be using to store country record data.

- **Analysis**: Analysis contains the spreadsheet analysis system you'll be developing in the next chapter.

- **Helper**: Helper contains information about the spreadsheet application. For example, it keeps track of how many total views there are in the wizard. It also keeps track of the current wizard page. In the next few chapters, it will keep track of even more.

The Input Wizard

The wizard used here has changed substantially from the previous chapter. In this section, I'll talk about some of those changes in design plus additional design enhancements. Figure 7-2 shows what your wizard looks like with all columns unhidden and zoomed out.

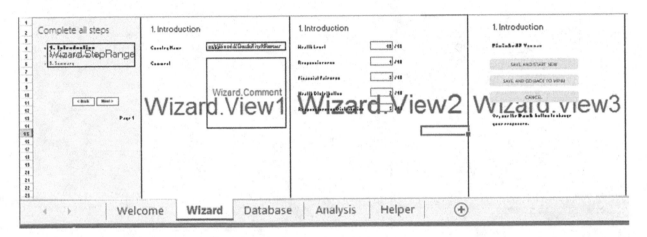

Figure 7-2. *All the different views of your wizard*

■ **Tip**   If you zoom out to 39%, the name of your named ranges will appear on top of the area to which they refer.

As in the previous chapter, the inputs of the wizard have each been given a name. Figure 7-3 shows the named ranges given for the inputs in the first view. Figure 7-4 shows the names for the inputs in the second view.

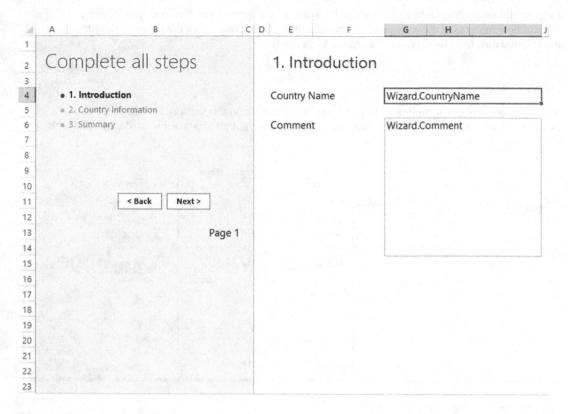

Figure 7-3. *Inputs on the first view*

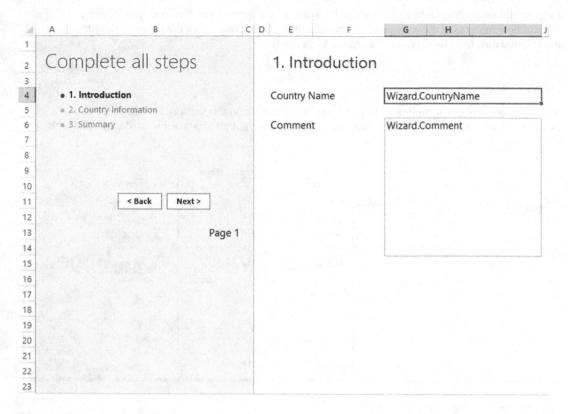

Figure 7-4. *Inputs on the second view*

If you ever need to change the location of these named ranges—or want to see where they are located immediately—you can use the Name Manager. Figure 7-5 shows the named ranges used to create spreadsheet-level variables. This keeps you from having to store everything in the code, which is error prone and not ideal.

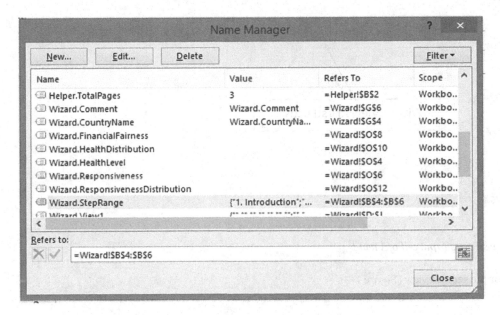

Figure 7-5. *The Name Manager showing all your spreadsheet variables*

Setting Focus to the First Input Cell

As the user clicks Next and Back in the wizard, one clear problem is that the selector doesn't move with it. For instance, if you are on the first screen, and the Comment box is selected (having just typed in some value), when you click Next, the selector will still be on the Comment box. What you want is for the selector to automatically focus on the top of each screen.

To do this, you'll set the first input box of each screen to follow the .FirstFocus pattern. For the first screen, you'll create a new named range called Wizard.View1.FirstFocus (Figure 7-6).

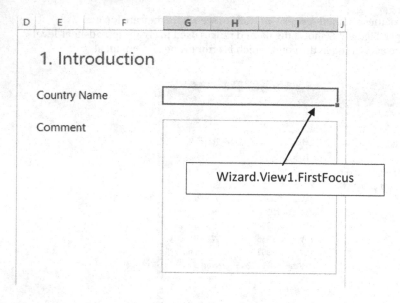

Figure 7-6. *Setting the .FirstFocus input cell of View 1*

You'll do the same for the second view (Figure 7-7).

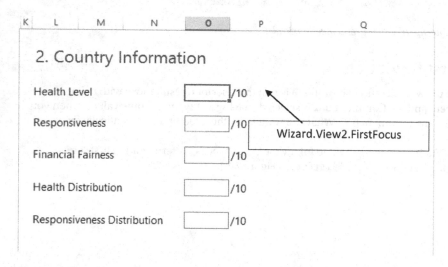

Figure 7-7. *Setting the FirstFocus for the second view*

You then need to adjust your GoNext and GoPrevious procedures, which are displayed in Listings 7-1 and 7-2.

Listing 7-1. The GoNext Procedure

```
Public Sub GoNext()
    Dim index As Integer

    ' Read in the current page index and increment it by one
    ' to go next
    index = [Helper.CurrentPageIndex]
    index = index + 1

    ' Check if we're already on the last page
    If index > [Helper.TotalPages] Then Exit Sub

    ' Unhide the next view
    Wizard.Range("Wizard.View" & index).Columns.Hidden = False
    SetFocusForView (index)

    ' Hide the current set of columns
    If index > 1 Then
        Wizard.Range("Wizard.View" & index - 1).Columns.Hidden = True
    End If

    'Set Helper.CurrentPageIndex equal to the next page index
    [Helper.CurrentPageIndex] = index
End Sub
```

Listing 7-2. The GoPrevious Procedure

```
Public Sub GoPrevious()
    Dim index As Integer

    ' Read in the current page index and decrement it by one
    ' to go previous
    index = [Helper.CurrentPageIndex]
    index = index - 1

    ' Check if we're already on the first page
    If index < 1 Then Exit Sub

    ' Unhide the previous view
    Wizard.Range("Wizard.View" & index).Columns.Hidden = False
    SetFocusForView (index)

    ' Hide the current set of columns
    If index < [Helper.TotalPages] Then
        Wizard.Range("Wizard.View" & index + 1).Columns.Hidden = True
    End If

    'Set Helper.CurrentPageIndex equal to the previous page index
    [Helper.CurrentPageIndex] = index
End Sub
```

The new procedure that helps you focus on the first input cell in each view is **`SetFocusForView`**, which is highlighted in bold in the code. The code for the `SetFocusForView` procedure is shown in Listing 7-3.

Listing 7-3. The SetFocusForView Procedure

```
Private Sub SetFocusForView(PageIndex As Integer)
    ' We test to ensure not on the last view of the wizard since
    ' there is nothing to focus in this view.
    If PageIndex < [Helper.TotalPages].Value Then
        Me.Range("Wizard.View" & PageIndex & ".FirstFocus").Activate
    End If
End Sub
```

Notice what `SetFocusForView` does. It takes in the current page number of the wizard. If you're looking at the first view, it looks for the named range `Wizard.View1.FirstFocus`. If you're on the second page, it looks for `Wizard.View2.FirstFocus`. Obviously, since you have only two pages with input (the third page gives the user a few buttons to make a choice), you need ensure you're not looking for a `.FirstFocus` cell where none exists on the page. Hence, you test to ensure you're not in the last view before doing anything.

Now let's take a moment to think about what you've built. In a broad sense, the code doesn't care too much about what page you're looking at so long as there is a `FirstFocus` on it. Moreover, if you make changes later, and want the `FirstFocus` to automatically start somewhere else, it's as simple as changing where the name points in the name manager. Third, because you're following a naming convention, it's fairly clear that `Wizard.View1.FirstFocus` refers to the first input cell in the first `View` on the Wizard tab. (Compare this to other naming conventions commonly in practice, which might have used something like `vw1_Focus1`). Finally, you see that named ranges are super flexible. A cell can have more than one named range pointing to it at any given time.

The Database

In this section, I'll talk about the interworkings of the database that serves to store user input. Figure 7-8 provides a snapshot of the database setup you'll be working with.

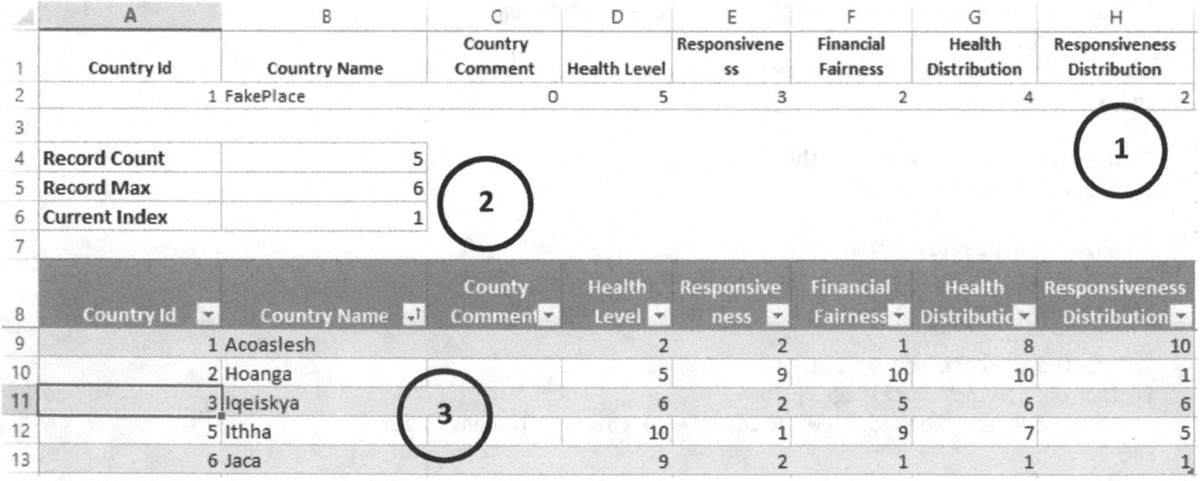

	A	B	C	D	E	F	G	H
1	Country Id	Country Name	Country Comment	Health Level	Responsiveness	Financial Fairness	Health Distribution	Responsiveness Distribution
2	1	FakePlace	0	5	3	2	4	2
3								
4	Record Count	5						
5	Record Max	6						
6	Current Index	1						
7								
8	Country Id	Country Name	County Comment	Health Level	Responsiveness	Financial Fairness	Health Distributio	Responsiveness Distribution
9	1	Acoaslesh		2	2	1	8	10
10	2	Hoanga		5	9	10	10	1
11	3	Iqeiskya		6	2	5	6	6
12	5	Iththa		10	1	9	7	5
13	6	Jaca		9	2	1	1	1

Figure 7-8. *The backend database storing country information filled in by the user*

Figure 7-8 shows that the database is made up of three components.

1. **Input Entry table**: Serves as the "living" record of current inputs from the wizard.

2. **Database Information table**: Keeps track of the different pieces of information required to add, edit, and delete records.

3. **Database table**: Keeps a record of all information stored currently in the database. I've aptly named this table "Database," which you can see by clicking into the table and going to the Design context menu.

Let's go through each section in detail.

Input Entry Table

The Input Entry table is what I like to call the "living record" of the current inputs from within the wizard. Figure 7-9 shows the actual formulas for the five metrics you're capturing beneath their values. Notice that they connect directly to the named ranges found in your wizard. Unfortunately, because of the size of named ranges and page size, I wasn't able to show full names, but you can readily understand what's going on here.

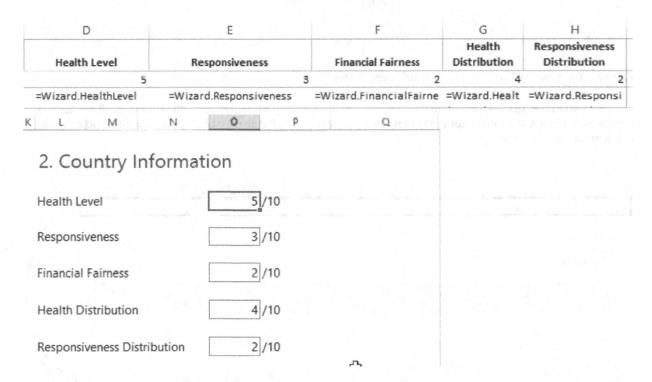

Figure 7-9. The values in the Input Entry table link directly to the cells on the wizard

The only cell that doesn't link directly is Country Id (Figure 7-10). I'll go into more detail on that in the next few sections.

	A	B
1	Country Id	Country Name
2	=INDEX(Database[Country Id],	Ithha
3	Database.CurrentIndex)	
4	**Record Count**	6
5	**Record Max**	7
6	**Current Index**	4
7		
8	Country Id ▼	Country Name ▼
9	1	Acoaslesh
10	2	Hoanga
11	3	Iqeiskya
12	5	Ithha
13	6	Jaca
14	7	FakePlace

Figure 7-10. *Country Id uses the current index and the table*

Once you have all the inputs from the wizard in one spot, adding it into the table can be done in fell swoop. You simply need to copy the values from the Input Entry table into your Database table. Figure 7-11 shows how you're going to do this conceptually.

	A	B	C	D	E	F	G	H	I
1	Country Id	Country Name	Country Comment	Health Level	Responsiveness	Financial Fairness	Health Distribution	Responsiveness Distribution	
2	-1	FakePlace		0	5	3	2	4	2
3									
4	**Record Count**	5							
5	**Record Max**	6							
6	**Current Index**	-1							
7									
8	Country Id ▼	Country Name ▼	County Comment ▼	Health Level ▼	Responsiveness ▼	Financial Fairness ▼	Health Distribution ▼	Responsiveness Distribution ▼	
9	1	Acoaslesh		2	2	1	8	10	
10	2	Hoanga		5	9	10	10	1	
11	3	Iqeiskya		6	2	5	6	6	
12	5	Ithha		10	1	9	7	5	
13	6	Jaca		9	2	1	1	1	
14									

Figure 7-11. *A conceptual visualization of how you add a new record to the database*

Because you don't want to do a lot of read/write action on the spreadsheet (since those are volatile), the best way to do this is to simply copy the information from the living record down to the bottom of the table. Figure 7-12 shows Input Entry completely filled in (the entire Input Entry row can be referred to by the named range Database.InputEntry). When you save a new record, the SaveNewRecord procedure is called. Listing 7-4 shows the code for this procedure.

| Database.InputEntry | | ▼ | : | ✕ | ✓ | *fx* | -1 | |

▲	A	B	C	D	E	F	G	H
1	Country Id	Country Name	Country Comment	Health Level	Responsiveness	Financial Fairness	Health Distribution	Responsiveness Distribution
2	-1	Fakeplace		0	5	3	2	4	2
3								
4	Record Count	6						
5	Record Max	7						
6	Current Index	-1						
7								
8	Country Id ▼	Country Name ▼ -1	County Comment ▼	Health Level ▼	Responsiveness ▼	Financial Fairness ▼	Health Distribution ▼	Responsiveness Distribution ▼
9	1	Acoaslesh		2	2	1	8	10
10	2	Hoanga		5	9	10	10	1
11	3	Iqeiskya		6	2	5	6	6
12	5	Ithha		10	1	9	7	5
13	6	Jaca		9	2	1	1	1
14	7	FakePlace		0	5	3	2	4	2

Figure 7-12. *The result of adding a new record*

Listing 7-4. The SaveNewRecord Procedure

```
Public Sub SaveNewRecord()
        Dim LastRowOfData       As Range
        Dim NewRowOfData        As Range
        Dim DatabaseRowCount    As Integer

        ' Find the last row in the Database table
        DatabaseRowCount = Database.ListObjects("Database").ListRows.Count
        Set LastRowOfData = Database.ListObjects("Database").ListRows(DatabaseRowCount).Range

        ' Find the next row to place the input entry
        Set NewRowOfData = LastRowOfData.Offset(1, 0)

        ' Place the new row of data
        NewRowOfData.Value = [Database.InputEntry].Value

        ' Set the ID of the new row of data with a new ID
        NewRowOfData(1, 1).Value = [Database.RecordMax].Value + 1
End Sub
```

What allows this code to work effectively is the use of Excel tables. A feature of these tables is their dynamic growth. When you add a new row of data right below its last record, it will subsume the new record. There's no extra VBA code required for this action to take place. It happens automatically. And here you'll use it to your advantage.

Your code finds the row count for all the data in the table. It then assigns the last row in the table to LastRowOfData. Next, you create a new range called NewRowOfData, which you tell Excel to place one row below the last. Next, you simply assign the NewRowOfData to be the same values as that of Database.InputEntry (one fell swoop, right?). Finally, you assign that new row of data a unique ID, which you'll go into the next section. Figure 7-12 shows the result of running the code.

Database Information Table

The Database Information table keeps track of all the information required to make changes to the Excel table. Figure 7-13 shows that the table is made up of three elements.

3		
4	Record Count	6
5	Record Max	7
6	Current Index	-1
7		

Figure 7-13. *The Database Information Table*

In this section, you'll go through them.

- Record Count keeps track of the total records in the database. It uses the formula =COUNT(Database[Country Id]).

- Record Max keeps track of the maximum Country Id of all countries listed. You need to keep track of the maximum Id for when you add records. The newest record will always be one plus the maximum record. This ensures each new record is always unique. The formula used is =MAX(Database[Country Id]).

- Current Index keeps track of whether you're editing a preexisting record or a new record. When Current Index equals negative one, you're editing a new record. Otherwise, when you're editing a preexisting record, Current Index will become the row index of the recording being edited.

The most important feature of Current Index is that it never refers to a Country Id. You may find this confusing at first, but it's a very important distinction. Figure 7-14 demonstrates this concept. In the Input Entry above, you see you're editing the country Ithha. Notice that while Country Id is five, Current Index is four. That's because Ithha is located in the fourth row down in your database table.

	A	B	C	D	E	F	G	H
1	Country Id	Country Name	Country Comment	Health Level	Responsiveness	Financial Fairness	Health Distribution	Responsiveness Distribution
2	5 Ithha		0	10	1	9	7	5
3								
4	Record Count	6						
5	Record Max	7						
6	Current Index	4						
7								
8	Country Id	Country Name	County Comment	Health Level	Responsiveness	Financial Fairness	Health Distribution	Responsiveness Distribution
9	1 Acoaslesh			2	2	1	8	10
10	2 Hoanga			5	9	10	10	1
11	3 Iqeiskya			6	2	5	6	6
12	5 Ithha			10	1	9	7	5
13	6 Jaca			9	2	1	1	1
14	7 FakePlace		0	5	3	2	4	2

Figure 7-14. *Ithha has a Country Id of 5 but the record index is 4*

You must separate location and Id. The reason is because later on in the chapter, you'll be sorting on country name (in fact, you can see it's already being sorted alphabetically in Figure 7-14). The location of the record could change with any update. In addition, you've also included the capability to delete records. Clearly, whatever country used to have a Country Id of 4 has been deleted from this table.

The Backend Database Table

Here you use one of Excel's most powerful capabilities—the table. There are several wonderful features of Excel tables that I'll talk about in this section. For one, they allow for easy dynamic range references (there's one exception to that, which I'll get into in the next section). If I want to include the Country Name column in an Index function, I need only supply Database[Country Name]. That reference to the Country Name column is also dynamic: this means I can add or remove records—and Excel will automatically reflect these changes in the Database[Country Name] reference.

Another great feature is the table's ability to expand to consume new entries. If I manually type in a new value in an unused cell directly adjacent to the table headings, Excel will expand to incorporate the new column heading. Likewise, if you add any data directly below the last record, the table will expand to consume the new record. The addition of new records is a boon to your development: you're able to add records to the database by simply writing to the spreadsheet. There's no extra overhead of grabbing the table object and inserting it. It's always best to let Excel handle the heavy lifting for you. It's not worth reinventing the wheel (perhaps I should say, "don't reinvent the pie chart," which is shaped like a wheel).

One other feature, which you will use in subsequent chapters, is the table's calculated columns feature. Figure 7-15 provides an example. In the first row, I've selected the Health Level response for reach country and added an arbitrary amount to it (for demonstration). Notice, the syntax used is the @ symbol. You can think of that @ symbol as telling Excel that you want to do something with the values in Health Level *at the same row* as the current formula. Pressing Enter on the formula will automatically fill the formula down to the end of the row. You can see by the result in Figure 7-15, that each value in Test Column has added two to the respective values of Health Level in the same row.

Health Level	Responsiveness	Financial Fairness	Health Distribution	Responsiveness Distribution	Test Column
2	2	1	8	10	=[@[Health Level]]+2
5	9	10	10	1	
6	2	5	6	6	
10	1	9	7	5	
9	2	1	1	1	
5	3	2	4	2	

Health Level	Responsiveness	Financial Fairness	Health Distribution	Responsiveness Distribution	Test Column
2	2	1	8	10	4
5	9	10	10	1	7
6	2	5	6	6	8
10	1	9	7	5	12
9	2	1	1	1	11
5	3	2	4	2	7

Figure 7-15. *A demonstration of calculated columns*

Menu Screen Functionality

Now let's focus on what's presented to the user when they first open the spreadsheet. Figure 7-16 shows the opening menu screen. In this section, I'll go through the different elements.

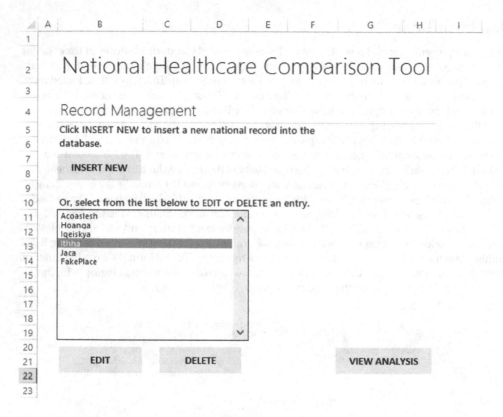

Figure 7-16. *The opening screen of your spreadsheet tool*

As you can see, the opening screen is made up of several different elements. The most prominent of those elements are Excel shapes and a ListBox form control. As stated earlier, I am not a fan of using form control buttons (that look like old Windows 95 buttons) on the spreadsheet. Rather, I much prefer using clean-looking Excel shapes and assigning macros to them.

Inserting a New Record

In this section, I'll talk about creating a new record *to be inserted* upon its completion. Here, I've created a button called Insert New Record. But this may be a misnomer since it doesn't insert a new record into the database; rather, it clears the wizard of its values and places the user on the wizard's first input screen. From the user's perspective, it prepares the wizard for the process of inserting a new record. See Listing 7-5.

Listing 7-5. The InsertNewRecord Procedure

```
Public Sub InsertNewRecord()
    Dim CurrentIndex As Integer

    'Set CurrentIndex to a new record
    [Database.CurrentIndex].Value = -1

    'Clear all inputs
    [Wizard.CountryName].Value = ""
    [Wizard.Comment].Value = ""
    [Wizard.HealthLevel].Value = ""
    [Wizard.Responsiveness].Value = ""
    [Wizard.FinancialFairness].Value = ""
    [Wizard.HealthDistribution].Value = ""
    [Wizard.ResponsivenessDistribution].Value = ""

    'Show the first page
    CurrentIndex = [Helper.CurrentPageIndex]
    Wizard.Range("Wizard.View" & CurrentIndex).Columns.Hidden = True
    Wizard.Range("Wizard.View1").Columns.Hidden = False
    [Helper.CurrentPageIndex].Value = 1

    'Activate the wizard
    Wizard.Activate
    SetFocusForView 1
End Sub
```

As with most of my code, I've attempted to the keep the logic fairly straightforward. You set the CurrentIndex to -1 to Excel when you're working with a new record. Next, you clear out any values in the table that may have been previously entered. Next, you tell Excel you want to start the user on the first page of entry. Finally, you activate the wizard to bring it into view.

Editing an Existing Record

In this section, I'll talk about how to edit an existing record. This is where the Current Index from the Database Information table comes in. Figure 7-17 shows the cell link for the ListBox actually pointing to Database.CurrentIndex. Recall the cell link tracks the row index for a selected item. Figure 7-18 shows that since you've selected the fourth row, your Current Index (stored as Database.CurrentIndex) is 4.

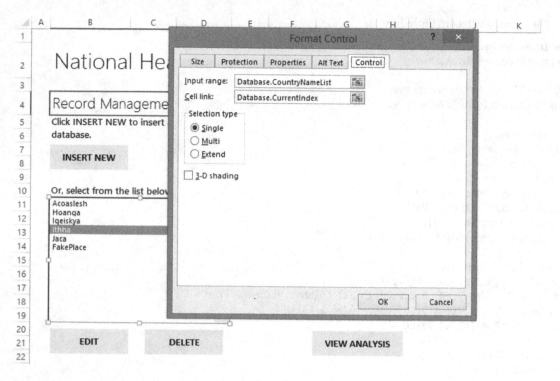

Figure 7-17. *Cell link refers to Database.CurrentIndex*

	A	B
1	Country Id	Country Name
2	5	0
3		
4	Record Count	6
5	Record Max	7
6	Current Index	4
7		

Figure 7-18. *Current Index is 4 because the list box on the front screen has the fourth row selected*

You now work in reverse of when you add a record to the table. Since you know the row location of the record you want to edit, you simply need to fill this information in your Input Entry table. Figure 7-19 shows what this looks like conceptually. Listing 7-6 provides the code for the procedure.

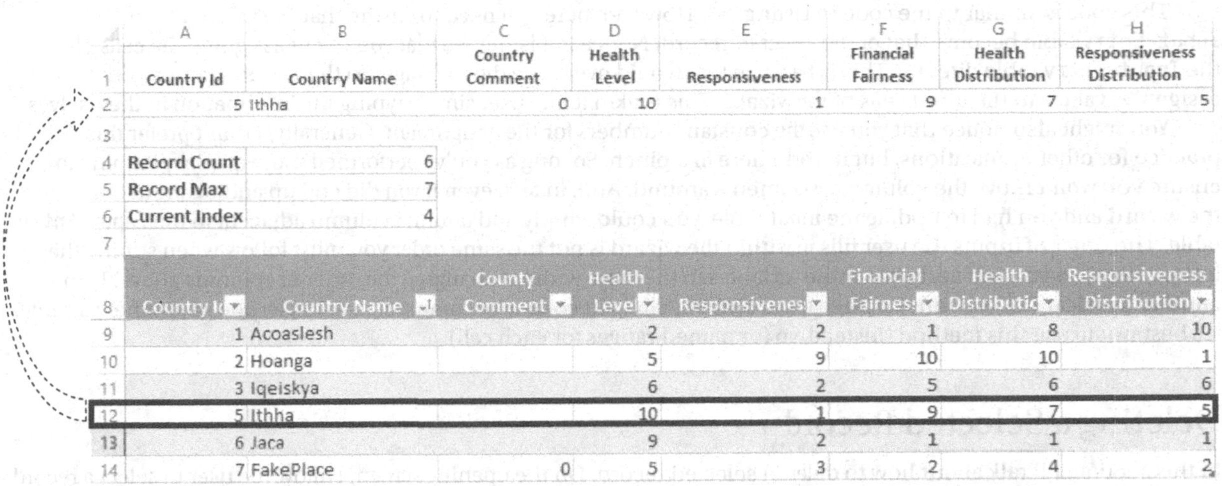

	A	B	C	D	E	F	G	H
1	Country Id	Country Name	Country Comment	Health Level	Responsiveness	Financial Fairness	Health Distribution	Responsiveness Distribution
2	5 Ithha		0	10		1	9	7	5
3								
4	Record Count	6						
5	Record Max	7						
6	Current Index	4						
7								
8	Country Id ▼	Country Name ▼	County Comment ▼	Health Level ▼	Responsivenes ▼	Financial Fairness ▼	Health Distributic ▼	Responsiveness Distribution ▼
9	1 Acoaslesh			2	2	1	8	10
10	2 Hoanga			5	9	10	10	1
11	3 Iqeiskya			6	2	5	6	6
12	5 Ithha			10	1	9	7	5
13	6 Jaca			9	2	1	1	1
14	7 FakePlace		0	5	3	2	4	2

Figure 7-19. *What happens when you edit a given record based on the user's selection in the list box from on the opening tab*

Listing 7-6. The EditSelectedRecord Procedure

```
Public Sub EditSelectedRecord()
    Dim CurrentSelectedIndex    As Integer
    Dim InputEntry              As Variant
    Dim CurrentIndex            As Integer


    ' Assign the currently selected index to CurrentSelectedIndex
    CurrentSelectedIndex = [Database.CurrentIndex]

    InputEntry = Database.ListObjects("Database").ListRows(CurrentSelectedIndex).Range

    [Wizard.CountryName].Value = InputEntry(1, 2)
    [Wizard.Comment].Value = InputEntry(1, 3)
    [Wizard.HealthLevel].Value = InputEntry(1, 4)
    [Wizard.Responsiveness].Value = InputEntry(1, 5)
    [Wizard.FinancialFairness].Value = InputEntry(1, 6)
    [Wizard.HealthDistribution].Value = InputEntry(1, 7)
    [Wizard.ResponsivenessDistribution].Value = InputEntry(1, 8)

    'Show the first page
    CurrentIndex = [Helper.CurrentPageIndex]
    Wizard.Range("Wizard.View" & CurrentIndex).Columns.Hidden = True
    Wizard.Range("Wizard.View1").Columns.Hidden = False
    [Helper.CurrentPageIndex].Value = 1

    'Activate the wizard
    Wizard.Activate
    SetFocusForView 1
End Sub
```

This code is similar to the code in Listing 7-5. However, here you need to ensure that the values of the `Input Entry` table become that of the selected record. Notice in Listing 7-6 that you're not assigning the cells of the `Input Entry` table directly. This is because that would overwrite their linkages to the wizard. Rather, you assign the values to the input cells of the wizard. This is akin to the user simply typing the information in themselves.

You might also notice that you use the constant numbers for the assignment. Generally, I don't prefer this practice for other applications, but it works here in a pinch. So long as you've performed the requisite planning to ensure you won't move the column assignments around. And, in fact, even if you did end up adding input boxes into the wizard and you had to update the input table, you could simply add another column adjacent to the `Input Entry` table. The order of inputs the user fills in within the wizard is not the same order you must follow when storing the information. So you can add even more variables to the store without changing the order of columns above. If, in another application, you must change these numbers in your code to accommodate the insertion of another variable, it's best not to use this method (instead, go for named ranges for each cell).

Deleting a Selected Record

In this section, I'll talk about how to delete a selected record. On the opening screen, I allow the user to select a record from the list box to be deleted. Listing 7-7 shows the code to delete a selected record.

Listing 7-7. The DeleteSelectedRecord Procedure.

```
Public Sub DeleteSelectedRecord()
    Dim CurrentSelectedIndex    As Integer

    ' Assign the currently selected index to CurrentSelectedIndex
    CurrentSelectedIndex = [Database.CurrentIndex]

    ' Move the ListBox Selector
    If [Database.CurrentIndex].Value = [Database.RecordCount] Then    'Last item on the list
        [Database.CurrentIndex].Value = [Database.CurrentIndex].Value - 1
    End If

    ' Delete the entry
    Database.ListObjects("Database").ListRows(CurrentSelectedIndex).Delete
End Sub
```

The code is fairly straightforward. You use the `CurrentIndex` to find the row location of the record you want to move. All you need to do is simply delete that row to remove it. The conditional in Listing 7-7 tests whether the selector is pointing to the last record in the table. If it is, you need to point it to the record that comes right before it since you'll be deleting that record. If you did not do this, `CurrentIndex` would continue to point to a record that no longer exists. You can see the problem this would cause by placing the selector on the last item in the list box. If you press Delete, the record is removed. If you pressed Delete again, an error would occur since the selector would point to a row location that is now greater than the total count of rows in the list.

Linking the Column of Country Names to the Form Control ListBox

In this section, I'll talk about how to automatically fill the list box with the list of country names from your backend database. Unfortunately, this is less straightforward than one might think. The problem stems from the ListBox's inability to accept a direct reference to the backend database. You might think you could just type `Database[Country Name]` into the `Input Range` of the form control's properties (refer to Figure 7-18). But doing this will generate a list box of blank data. Therefore, you need to create a dynamically sized named range using good ol' fashioned functions.

Look back at Figure 7-18, and you can see you've specified the named range `Database.CountryNameList`. Let's take a look at its formula.

```
=INDEX(Database[Country Name],1):INDEX(Database[Country Name],Database.RecordCount)
```

In previous chapters, I talked about creating dynamically sized functions such as these. The range operator (the colon) is what makes this formula work so seamlessly. Let's look at Figure 7-20 while attempting to go through this function. The left side of the function `INDEX(Database[Country Name],1)` will always return the first record in the `Country Name` column of your table—cell B9 in Figure 7-19. The right side, `INDEX(Database[Country Name], Database.RecordCount)`, will always return the last record in the table—cell B14 in Figure 7-20. Remember that Excel treats what `INDEX` returns as a cell reference, so behind the scenes Excel constructs the range B9:B14 on the fly based on this formula. If you added a record, Excel would construct the effective range B9:B15 on the fly.

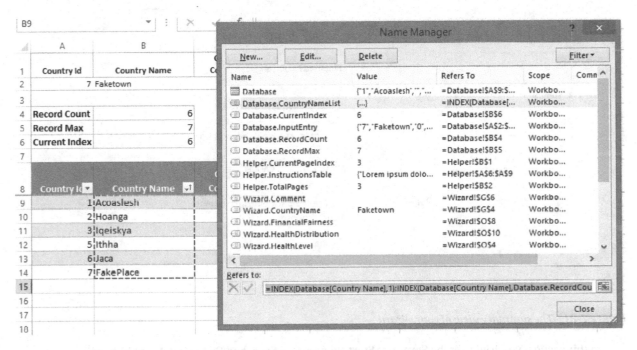

Figure 7-20. Dynamic formulas help you construct this dynamic range on the fly

Looking back to Figure 7-16, it's a matter of simply linking the ListBox's input Range to this dynamic range.

The final button on the opening menu takes users to the analysis page. I'll go over that in more detail in the next two chapters. In the meantime, look at the excerpted code in Listing 7-8. (Note this code is located in the Welcome sheet object.)

Listing 7-8. The GoToAnalysis Procedure

```
Public Sub GoToAnalysis()
    Analysis.Activate
End Sub
```

Wizard Summary Buttons

Now let's focus on the buttons that appear in the third, summary view of your wizard (see Figure 7-21). In this section, you'll go through each of these buttons. Here's a quick summary of what they do:

- **Save, and Start New**: Saves the current input and begins a new record from page 1 of the wizard.

- **Save, and Go Back To Menu**: Saves the current record and returns the user to the menu screen.

- **Cancel**: Does nothing with the current record and simply returns the user to the menu screen.

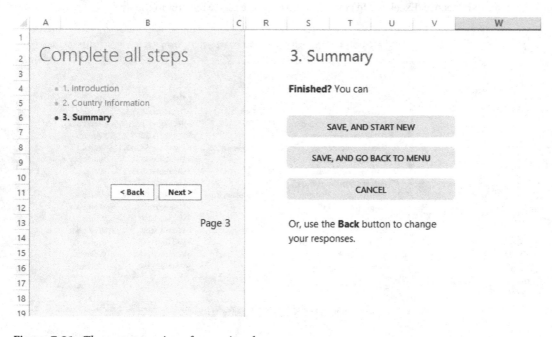

Figure 7-21. *The summary view of your wizard*

In this section, you'll go over the **Save, and Start New** and the **Save, and Go Back to Menu** buttons. Listings 7-9 and 7-10 show their code, respectively.

Listing 7-9. The SaveAndStartNew Procedure

```
Public Sub SaveAndStartNew()
    Dim CurrentIndexOfRecord As Integer

    CurrentIndexOfRecord = [Database.CurrentIndex].Value
    If CurrentIndexOfRecord = -1 Then
        Wizard.SaveNewRecord
    Else
        Wizard.SaveSelectedRecord (CurrentIndexOfRecord)
    End If
    Database.SortCountryNames
    Wizard.InsertNewRecord
End Sub
```

Listing 7-10. The SaveAndGoBackToMenu Procedure

```
Public Sub SaveAndGoBackToMenu()
    Dim CurrentIndexOfRecord As Integer

    CurrentIndexOfRecord = [Database.CurrentIndex].Value
    If CurrentIndexOfRecord = -1 Then
        Wizard.SaveNewRecord
    Else
        Wizard.SaveSelectedRecord (CurrentIndexOfRecord)
    End If

    Database.SortCountryNames
    Wizard.GoToMenu
End Sub
```

Notice that both of these procedures perform the same functions. First, they test if the Current Index is -1. Again, you know if it's -1 you're dealing with a new record. Therefore, you call SaveNewRecord (Listing 7-4, from earlier in the chapter). Otherwise, you're dealing with a record that already exists. In that case, you call SaveSelectedRecord (Listing 7-11).

Listing 7-11. The SaveSelectedRecord Procedure

```
Public Sub SaveSelectedRecord(RecordIndex)
    Dim SelectedRowOfData As Range

    ' Assign SelectedRowOfData to the index in the database
    ' corresponding to the record we're editing
    Set SelectedRowOfData = Database.ListObjects("Database").ListRows(RecordIndex).Range

    ' Assign the updated entries back to the selected row
    SelectedRowOfData.Value = [Database.InputEntry].Value
End Sub
```

The SaveSelectedRecord procedure works similarly to that of SaveNewRecord. However, because the record already exists on the table, you need not doing anything additional except set the values in the row location to those of the Input Entry table.

Returning to Listing 7-9 and 7-10, both procedures call the Database.SortCountryNames (Listing 7-12). As you make updates to the table, you want to keep the integrity of an alphabetical sort. Here, you use a simple command to the table to resort the data using the CountryName column. Note this procedure is actually in the Database sheet object (which is why you use Database.SortCountryNames).

Listing 7-12. The SortCountryNames Procedure

```
Public Sub SortCountryNames()
    Me.ListObjects("Database").Sort.SortFields.Add Key:=[Database[Country Name]]
End Sub
```

Finally, returning once again to Listings 7-9 and 7-10, you see two both procedures differ with respect to their last line of code (which I've bolded). In Listing 7-9, you want to start the wizard over and insert another record. So you call InsertNewRecord (Listing 7-5). On the other hand, Listing 7-10 takes you back to the menu, so you call GoToMenu (Listing 7-13). Likewise, the Cancel button shown in Figure 7-21 calls GoToMenu directly.

Listing 7-13. The GoToMenuProcedure

```
Public Sub GoToMenu()
    Welcome.Activate
End Sub
```

The Last Word

In this chapter, you built upon the wizard from the previous chapter. You developed a backend database system that works seamlessly when complete. Whenever available, you let Excel do the work for you—by using formulas and features inherent to Excel's tables. You also used quite a bit of code, but you were careful to make your code simple and readable. Specifically, you avoided using code for everything. By creating a proper balance between code, formulas, and features, you've built the beginnings of a robust Excel application. And that's thinking outside the cell.

CHAPTER 8

∎∎∎

Building for Sensitivity Analysis

In the previous chapters, you investigated a wizard that could take in and store user input. In this chapter, you're going to create a dashboard that allows you to perform sensitivity analysis based on the metrics described in the previous chapter. Figure 8-1 provides a preview of what's to come.

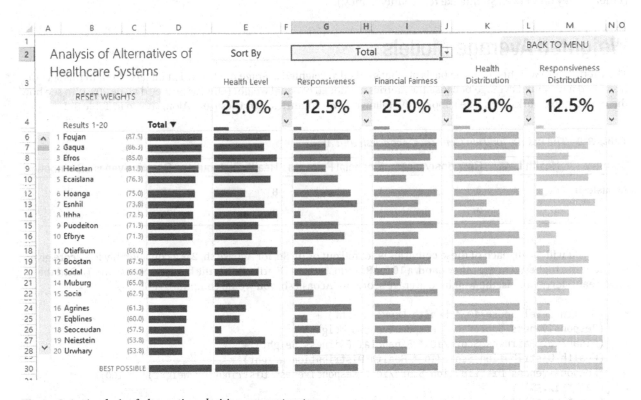

Figure 8-1. *Analysis of alternatives decision support system*

The tool shown in Figure 8-1 allows you to do many things quickly and efficiently, much of it with only a small amount of VBA code. As you'll see, many of the mechanics are driven by Excel's built-in functions, like conditional formatting and formulas. The correct combination between formulas and code here is key. It's what allows you to make instantaneous updates to the data without the need of a "recalculate" button.

But before you do anything, let's return to the metrics described in the previous chapter. See Table 8-1.

Table 8-1. *Metrics Used by the World Health Organization's Study*

Metric	Description	Weight
Health Level	Measures life expectancy for a given country.	25.0%
Responsiveness	Measures factors such as speed to health service, access to doctors, et al.	12.5%
Financial Fairness	Measures the fairness of who shoulders the burden of financial costs in a country.	25%
Health Distribution	Measures the level of equitable distribution of healthcare in a country.	25%
Responsiveness Distribution	Measures the level of equitable distribution of responsiveness defined above.	12%
		100%

Source: The World Health Report 2000 - Health Systems: Improving Performance (www.who.int/whr/2000/en/)

The weights described herein are in fact the same weights the World Health Organization used in its original study. However, as mentioned in the previous chapter, the data you have is notional and the countries are fakes (I mean, they don't even sound like real county names!).

Weighted Average Models

The metrics and weights form the basis of what's called a weighted average model, which I'll talk about in this section. It's called a weighted average because the metrics are not all of equal weight (otherwise, they'd all be 20%). To see how the whole thing works, let's take a look at the following two countries, Acoaslesh and Afon, shown in Table 8-2.

Table 8-2. *The Results for Two Countries, Acoaslesh and Afon*

Country	Health Level	Responsiveness	Financial Fairness	Health Distribution	Responsiveness Distribution
Acoaslesh	2	2	1	8	10
Afon	4	2	4	2	3

As you will recall, each of these countries is scored out of 10. So, for Acoaslesh, 2 is a considerably low score given that 10 is the highest. On the other hand, a 10 for Responsiveness Distribution is the best possible score. To find the total health level (that is, the weighted average score) for Acoaslesh, you would compute as follows:

```
= [(Health Level Score/10 * Health Level Weight) +
   (Responsiveness Score/10 * Responsiveness Weight) +
   (Financial Fairness Score/10 * Financial Fairness Weight) +
   (Health Distribution Score/10 * Health Distribution Weight) +
   (Responsiveness Distribution Score/10 * Responsiveness Distribution Weight)] * 100
= [(.20 * 12.5%) +
   (.20 * 25.0%) +
   (.10 * 25.0%) +
   (.80 * 25.0%) +
   (1.00 * 12.5%)] * 100
```

```
= .425 * 100 = 42.5.
```

So for Acoaslesh, the overall health score is .425, where 1 is now the best score. That process of taking the scores and making them proportionate to the scale of 0 to 1 is called normalization.

Sometimes it's easier to understand these final scores as being out of 100 instead. So let's scale .425 to be 42.5 by multiplying the result by 100. Whether you choose .425 or 42.5, both answers are correct. It's up to you how you want to present the numbers to your audience.

Likewise, you can perform the same calculations for Afon.

$$= \ [(.40 * 12.5\%) +$$
$$(.20 * 25.0\%) +$$
$$(.40 * 25.0\%) +$$
$$(.20 * 25.0\%) +$$
$$(.30 * 12.5\%)] * 100$$

$$= 28.8$$

By scaling to 100, you make the perfect score any country could get 100 (again, if you don't scale, the perfect score is 1). You can see this yourself by assuming perfect 10s across the board and doing the calculations. When you do this for each country, you'll come up with a list like the one below. This allows you to say the countries ranking higher are better performers *according to your model* than the ones below (Figure 8-2).

8	Country Name ▼	Total ↲
9	Foujan	87.5
10	Efros	83.8
11	Gaqua	82.5
12	Hoanga	80.0
13	Heiestan	78.8
14	Esnhil	76.3
15	Ecaislana	73.8
16	Efbrye	73.8
17	Boostan	71.3
18	Puodeiton	71.3
19	Agrines	66.3
20	Sodal	62.5
21	Ithha	61.3
22	Seoceudan	61.3
23	Socia	61.3
24	Otiaflium	60.0
25	Eqblines	57.5
26	Muburg	55.0

Figure 8-2. A rank of country performance based on the weighted average model

---

■ **Note**   The statistician George E. P. Box once remarked, "All models are wrong, some are useful." You should always remember models are simplifications (sometimes even gross over-simplifications) of reality. By their nature, they cannot capture everything. Indeed, this was a criticism of the World Health Organization regarding the these metrics; some argued that other factors were not correctly captured or weighted. Therefore, it's important to be specific when discussing model results. Rather than assert the validity of the results as being unequivocal truth, remember they are the product of a series of assumptions.

Sensitivity Analysis on a Weighted Average Model

In this section, I'll talk about sensitivity analysis with respect to the weights for a given country. The weighted sum model presented is used to evaluate many different countries. Broadly, you're simply investigating a resultant list of countries whose *scores* follow directly from the *importance* of each metric (given by its weight) in your model. As such, you may want to investigate how changing the importance of inputs impacts overall scores. This is called *sensitivity analysis*.

One-Way Sensitivity Analysis

One simple, if powerful, sensitivity analysis method is to vary only one weight at a time while maintaining the proportional importance of the other weights. This is called *one-way sensitivity analysis* and it works like this. Let's say you want to see what happens if you increase Health Level by 4%. First, let's divide the weight into two theoretical groups (Figure 8-3).

WHAT WE WANT TO CHANGE HEALTH LEVEL	HEALTH DISTRIBUTION	WHAT WE WANT TO MAINTAIN RESPONSIVENESS	RESPONSIVENESS DISTRIBUTION	FINANCIAL FAIRNESS	SUM TOTAL
25.0%	25.0%	12.5%	12.5%	25.0%	100.0%
=		=			
25%		75%			100.0%

Figure 8-3.   *The weights split into two groups based upon which weights you want to change and which you want to maintain*

The rule here is that each group must always sum to 100%. So, if you add 4% to Health Level, you have to subtract it from the other group (see Figure 8-4).

	Beginning	Change	New %
HEALTH LEVEL	25%	4%	29%
OTHER GROUP	75%	-4%	71%
	100%		100%

Figure 8-4. *If you add 4% to one group, you must remove it from the other*

Now that the overall sum of the "other group" has changed, the weights that make up that group are adjusted while maintaining the same proportion to the group's sum as they did before. In this next stage, you find the new proportions for the group you want to maintain (Figure 8-5).

	HEALTH DISTRIBUTION	RESPONSIVENESS	RESPONSIVENESS DISTRIBUTION	FINANCIAL FAIRNESS
Original Weight	25.0%	12.5%	12.5%	25.0%
Divide by old group sum	75.0%	75.0%	75.0%	75.0%
Proportion	**33.3%**	**16.7%**	**16.7%**	**33.3%**

Figure 8-5. *Finding the new proportions for the group you want to maintain*

In the next step, you multiply each calculated proportion by the new group weight (Figure 8-6).

	HEALTH DISTRIBUTION	RESPONSIVENESS	RESPONSIVENESS DISTRIBUTION	FINANCIAL FAIRNESS
Proportion	33.3%	16.7%	16.7%	33.3%
Multiply by new group weight	71.0%	71.0%	71.0%	71.0%
New Weight	**23.7%**	**11.8%**	**11.8%**	**23.7%**

Figure 8-6. *Multiply the new proportions by the new group weight*

Finally, you reassign the new weights to their metrics (Figure 8-7). If you add all the weights together, they now once again sum to 100%.

HEALTH LEVEL	HEALTH DISTRIBUTION	RESPONSIVENESS	RESPONSIVENESS DISTRIBUTION	FINANCIAL FAIRNESS
29.0%	23.7%	11.8%	11.8%	23.7%

Figure 8-7. *New metrics weights*

In this chapter, I'll talk about how to build this mechanism into your spreadsheet. I've devised a method that I call Easy One-Way Sensitivity Analysis. You'll be surprised how easy it is to implement into your application. Indeed, you can take advantage of Excel's form controls to help you do much of the heavy lifting. That said, there are a few limitations with this method, and I'll go over them in this chapter.

Creating a Linked Values Table

In this section, I'll describe how to create the Easy One-Way Sensitivity Analysis mechanism and implement it in the spreadsheet application from the previous chapter. If you upload Chapter8Wizard.xlsm, we're starting on the Helper tab.

In Figure 8-8, I've placed five scroll bar form controls onto the spreadsheet, one for each metric. I've then linked each scroll bar to a cell on the right of each metric under the column Linked Value. Just for clarification, the left-most scroll bar links to cell B5, and the right-most links to cell B9. As you can see in Figure 8-3, the middle scroll bar is linked to Financial Fairness, B7.

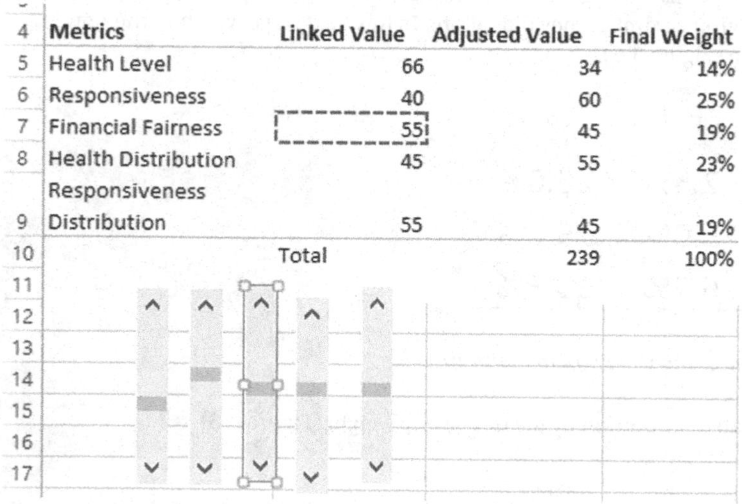

Metrics	Linked Value	Adjusted Value	Final Weight
Health Level	66	34	14%
Responsiveness	40	60	25%
Financial Fairness	55	45	19%
Health Distribution	45	55	23%
Responsiveness Distribution	55	45	19%
Total		239	100%

Figure 8-8. *Setting the scrollbars to the their linked cells*

For each scroll bar, I've set its minimum value to 1 and its maximum value to 100. Figure 8-9 shows an example.

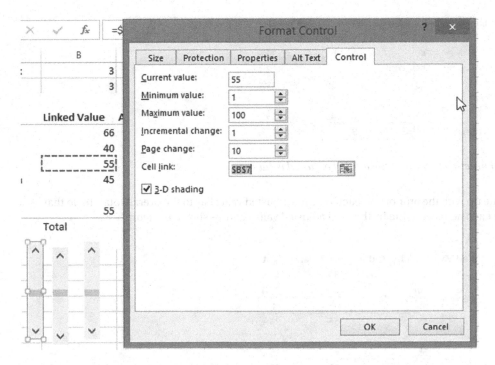

Figure 8-9. *Each scroll bar has a minimum of 1 and a maximum of 0. Right-click the scroll bar and select format control to see this property window*

Recall from previous chapters how form control scroll bars work. The more you scroll down, the greater the number in the linked cell. While there's nothing wrong with that per se, it's counterintuitive for some users. For your purposes, you'd like the action of scrolling up to actually increase the resulting value and scrolling down to decrease. So you need to adjust the values on the spreadsheet to reflect this preference.

Insert another column next to Linked Values and call it Adjusted Values. In each cell next to the linked values, you'll take the scroll bar's value and subtract it from 100 (the max value of the scroll bar). Figure 8-10 shows this formula.

	Metrics	Linked Value	Adjusted Value	Final Weight
4				
5	Health Level	66	=100-B5	14%
6	Responsiveness	40	60	25%
7	Financial Fairness	55	45	19%
8	Health Distribution	45	55	23%
9	Responsiveness Distribution	55	45	19%
10		Total	239	100%
11				

Figure 8-10. *Now, as you scroll down, the Adjusted Value decreases. As you scroll up, the Adjusted Value increases*

Next, you need to add to find the grand total of all the adjusted values. You can do that by adding a SUM cell at the bottom of the Adjusted Value column (see Figure 8-11).

4	Metrics	Linked Value	Adjusted Value	Final Weight
5	Health Level	66	34	14%
6	Responsiveness	40	60	25%
7	Financial Fairness	55	45	19%
8	Health Distribution	45	55	23%
9	Responsiveness Distribution	55	45	19%
10		Total	=SUM(C5:C9)	100%

Figure 8-11. *Use the SUM function to the find the total of adjusted values*

Now you want to come up with the proportion each metric's adjusted value has to the overall total. To do that, you simply need to divide each adjusted value by the total adjusted value sum, as shown in Figure 8-12.

4	Metrics	Linked Value	Adjusted Value	Final Weight
5	Health Level	66	34	14%
6	Responsiveness	40	60	25%
7	Financial Fairness	55	45	=C7/$C$10
8	Health Distribution	45	55	23%
9	Responsiveness Distribution	55	45	19%
10		Total	239	100%

Figure 8-12. *Find the final weight by dividing each adjusted value by the total adjusted value*

And that's it! If you play around with the scroll bars, you can change the weights as much as you want. The final weight will always equal 100%! Figure 8-13 shows an adjustment to the scroll bar assigned to Health Level.

4	Metrics	Linked Value	Adjusted Value	Final Weight
5	Health Level	84	16	8%
6	Responsiveness	60	40	20%
7	Financial Fairness	51	49	24%
8	Health Distribution	45	55	27%
9	Responsiveness Distribution	55	45	22%
10		Total	205	100%
11				
12				
13				
14				
15				
16				
17				

Figure 8-13. *No matter what values are assigned to the scroll bar, the final weights will always add up to 100%*

Linking to the Database

You're now interested in how you can link the one-way sensitivity analysis mechanism back into the database. The first thing you want to do is give each of these weights a name. Figure 8-14 shows them named following my usual conventions.

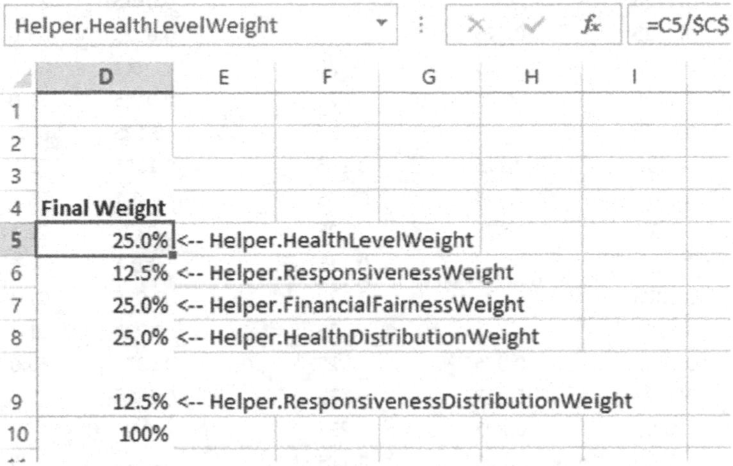

Figure 8-14. *Each final weight is named in the Linked Values table*

In the Database tab, I've added a few extra columns that reflect the operations you must do for each metric for each country in your list (see Figure 8-15). Across the top of the new columns, I've included a reference to the actual weight values for each metric. This isn't technically necessary, as you'll see. However, I think it provides a good reference into understanding the calculations. Anything you can do to make your work easier to understand when you come back to it is, in my opinion, always worthwhile.

=Helper.HealthLevelWeight		weights				
		12.50%	25.00%	25.00%	12.50%	
Health Level (weighted) ▼	▼	Responsiveness (weighted) ▼	Financial Fairness (weighted) ▼	Health Distribution (weighted) ▼	Responsiveness Distribution (weighted) ▼	Total ▼↓
3	0.225	0.1125	0.25	0.25	0.0375	87.5
5	0.25	0.1125	0.225	0.2	0.0625	85.0
8	0.2	0.0625	0.25	0.25	0.1	86.3
1	0.125	0.1125	0.25	0.25	0.0125	75.0
10	0.175	0.0625	0.2	0.25	0.125	81.3
9	0.2	0.125	0.175	0.125	0.1125	73.8
8	0.225	0.0875	0.125	0.225	0.1	76.3
3	0.15	0.1	0.175	0.25	0.0375	71.3
8	0.125	0.1	0.225	0.125	0.1	67.5
2	0.175	0.0875	0.25	0.175	0.025	71.3
2	0.125	0.1125	0.1	0.25	0.025	61.3
7	0.175	0.0625	0.075	0.25	0.0875	65.0
5	0.25	0.0125	0.225	0.175	0.0625	72.5
4	0.025	0.05	0.225	0.225	0.05	57.5
5	0.1	0.0375	0.25	0.175	0.0625	62.5
2	0.25	0.0375	0.15	0.225	0.025	68.8
2	0.1	0.025	0.225	0.225	0.025	60.0

Figure 8-15. *The weights across the top correspond to the weights you developed on the Helper tab*

■ **Tip**   You should develop with the future in mind. Ask yourself, will you understand what's going on when you come back to your spreadsheet having not seen it in three months?

Note that each of the new columns corresponding to the metrics now has "(weighted)" added to the name. This is because these columns represent the individual scores divided by 10 and multiplied by their corresponding weight on the Helper tab. Figure 8-16 shows the formula used for Health Level (weighted).

✕ ✓ *fx* | =[@[Health Level]]/10*Helper.HealthLevelWeight

	I	J	K	L	M
			weights		
	25.00%	12.50%	25.00%	25.00%	12.50%
▼	Health Level (weighted) ▼	Responsiveness (weighted) ▼	Financial Fairness (weighted) ▼	Health Distribution (weighted) ▼	Responsiveness Distribution (weighted) ▼
3	=[@[Health Level]]	0.1125	0.25	0.25	0.0375
5	0.25	0.1125	0.225	0.2	0.0625

Figure 8-16. *Each weighted column takes the original scored value, divides it by ten, and then multiplies it by its respective weight from the Helper tab*

Finally, the Total column is simply the sum of all weights (see Figure 8-17).

	I	J	K	L	M	N
	× ✓ *fx*	=SUM(Database[@[Health Level (weighted)]:[Responsiveness Distribution (weighted)]])*100				
			weights			
	25.00%	12.50%	25.00%	25.00%	12.50%	
	Health Level (weighted)	Responsiveness (weighted)	Financial Fairness (weighted)	Health Distribution (weighted)	Responsiveness Distribution (weighted)	Total
3	0.225	0.1125	0.25	0.25	0.0375	=SUM(Dat

Figure 8-17. *The Total column is simply the sum of all the weighted scores*

You may not have realized it, but you've just built the infrastructure for one-way sensitivity analysis! If you go back to the descriptions of weighted average models and one-way sensitivity analysis from the beginning of this chapter, you'll see that you've re-created the algebra step-by-step.

Building the Tool

In this section, I'll talk about what the new tool does and how to build the functionality. I'll be going piece by piece, so let's get started.

Getting to the Backend, the Intermediate Table

As you know, I'm a huge fan of intermediate tables. We almost always need to transform (that is, do something to) the data before presenting it to the user. Obviously, where you place your intermediate tables is up to you. For many projects, I prefer placing them on a new tab. But sometimes when dealing with something that's complicated, I like to place the table in the same worksheet tab as the decision support system or dashboard. That's what I've done here.

If you look at the Analysis tab in your file, you'll see that the rows beyond 28 are hidden. That's because your intermediate table is somewhere in the hidden rows. So the first thing you'll want to do is unhide all rows to get a peek at the intermediate table. The easiest way to do that, in my opinion, is to click the grey triangle at the upper left of your worksheet to select everything (of course, there's always CTRL+A). Then from on the Home tab, go to Format ➤ Hide & Unhide ➤ Unhide rows. Figure 8-18 shows these steps.

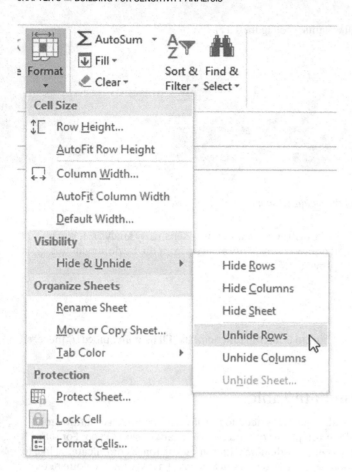

Figure 8-18. *Steps to unhide rows*

The intermediate table is shown in Figure 8-19.

Intermediate Table

| Scrollbar Value | 1 |
| Sort Column Id | 6 |

#	Sort Column: Total	Match Index	Country	1 Health Level	2 Responsiveness	3 Financial Fairness	4 Health Distribution	5 Responsiveness Distribution	6 Total
1	87.5027	14	Foujan	90	90	100	100	30	87.50
2	86.2533	15	Gaqua	80	50	100	100	80	86.25
3	85.0002	9	Efros	100	90	90	80	50	85.00
4	81.2525	16	Heiestan	70	50	80	100	100	81.25
5	76.2550	7	Ecaislana	90	70	50	90	80	76.25
6	75.0015	17	Hoanga	50	90	100	100	10	75.00
7	73.7548	13	Esnhil	80	100	70	50	90	73.75
8	72.5038	19	Ithha	100	10	90	70	50	72.50
9	71.2519	30	Puodeiton	70	70	100	70	20	71.25
10	71.2516	8	Efbrye	60	80	70	100	30	71.25
11	68.7510	27	Otiaflium	100	30	60	90	20	68.75
12	67.5037	5	Boostan	50	80	90	50	80	67.50
13	65.0013	37	Sodal	70	50	30	100	70	65.00
14	65.0001	22	Muburg	90	10	40	90	70	65.00
15	62.5003	36	Socia	40	30	100	70	50	62.50
16	61.2512	3	Agrines	50	90	40	100	20	61.25
17	60.0036	12	Eqblines	40	20	90	90	20	60.00
18	57.5029	35	Seoceudan	10	40	90	90	40	57.50
19	53.7535	23	Neiestein	80	30	20	50	100	53.75
20	53.7526	39	Urwhary	70	40	50	60	30	53.75
			Is Sorted On?	FALSE	FALSE	FALSE	FALSE	FALSE	TRUE

Figure 8-19. *The intermediate table*

What each element of this table does may not be immediately clear. In the next few sections, I'll go through the functionality of the dashboard. You will see where those functionalities tie in directly to the items on the intermediate table.

Scrolling Capability

In this section, I'll talk about how you achieve this scrolling capability. Recall the dynamic table built previously.We want the same functionality here. Hopefully, by now you're very familiar with the scroll bar (maybe even be sick of it!). In this current example decision tool, you will again use this dynamic.

As Figure 8-20 shows, you've simply inserted a new scroll bar into the sheet and linked it to the cell adjacent to Scrollbar Value. This cell contains the current value of the scroll bar.

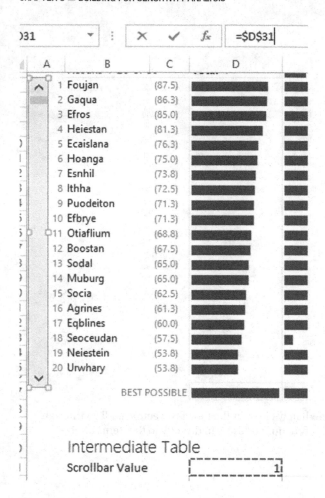

Figure 8-20. *The scroll bar for the table presented to the user is linked to a cell on your intermediate table*

As is typically the case for a scrolling table, the first cell in the table is always equal to the scroll bar value. Each cell below it is then equal to one plus the cell above. Therefore, as the scroll bar changes, each cell below changes in tandem. Figure 8-21 shows this conceptually. Figure 8-22 shows the actual formulas.

	A	B	C	D
30	Intermediate Table			
31	Scrollbar Value			1
32	Sort Column Id			6
		Sort Column:	Match	
33	#	Total	Index	Country
34	1	87.5027	14	Foujan
35	2	86.2533	15	Gaqua
36	3	85.0002	9	Efros
37	4	81.2525	16	Heiestan
38	=A37+1		7	Ecaislana
39	6	75.0015	17	Hoanga
40	7	73.7548	13	Esnhil
41	8	72.5038	19	Ithha
42	9	71.2519	30	Puodeiton
43	10	71.2516	8	Efbrye
44	11	68.7510	27	Otiaflium
45	12	67.5037	5	Boostan
46	13	65.0013	37	Sodal
47	14	65.0001	22	Muburg
48	15	62.5003	36	Socia
49	16	61.2512	3	Agrines
50	17	60.0036	12	Eqblines
51	18	57.5029	35	Seoceudan
52	19	53.7535	23	Neiestein
53	20	53.7526	39	Urwhary

Figure 8-21. *The scrolling table dynamic shown conceptually*

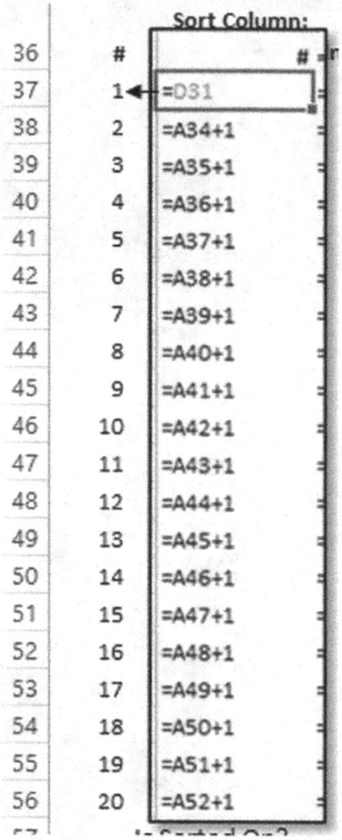

		Sort Column:	
36	#		#
37	1	=O31	
38	2	=A34+1	
39	3	=A35+1	
40	4	=A36+1	
41	5	=A37+1	
42	6	=A38+1	
43	7	=A39+1	
44	8	=A40+1	
45	9	=A41+1	
46	10	=A42+1	
47	11	=A43+1	
48	12	=A44+1	
49	13	=A45+1	
50	14	=A46+1	
51	15	=A47+1	
52	16	=A48+1	
53	17	=A49+1	
54	18	=A50+1	
55	19	=A51+1	
56	20	=A52+1	

Figure 8-22. *Cells A34:A50 from above with only their formulas showing*

Notice that the index numbers from the visual presentation section of your tool are directly linked to the index numbers from below the sheet (see Figure 8-23).

Figure 8-23. The intermediate table links directly to the visual presentation section

Adjusting the Scroll Bar

In this section, I'll talk about making adjustments to the scroll bar. By default, all form control scroll bars start with a minimum value of zero and go to 100. In your case, you'll never use the zero, so you need to adjust the minimum to always be 1. Another issue is that you expect the size of the list to change. The current example database has about 30 data items in it. But you need to accommodate an ever-changing range of data. The only instances in which you expect the amount of entries to change is when you either add or delete a new item.

At the end of both the InsertNewRecord and DeleteSelectedRecord procedures I've added a call to SetScrollbarMax. Listing 8-1 shows the code for this procedure.

Listing 8-1. SetScrollbarMax

```
Private Sub SetScrollbarMax()
    If [Database.RecordCount].Value <= 20 Then
        Analysis.Shapes("Analysis.Scrollbar").ControlFormat.Enabled = False
    Else
        Analysis.Shapes("Analysis.Scrollbar").ControlFormat.Enabled = True
        Analysis.Shapes("Analysis.Scrollbar").ControlFormat.Max =
            [Database.RecordCount].Value - 20 + 1
    End If

    Analysis.Shapes("Analysis.Scrollbar").ControlFormat.Value = 1
End Sub
```

The code works like this: you have 20 entries you can display on the visual layer (that's just the number I've picked, but it may be different in your own work). When the record count is greater than 20, you always want the scroll bar max to be 19 (one less than the total amount you're showing) less than that total (the chapter on form controls talks about why this is). On the other hand, if the RecordCount is less than 20, you won't need the scroll bar at all so you can just disable it. Finally, it's always a good idea to reset the scroll position whenever there's a change.

Formula-based Sorting Data for Analysis

In Figure 8-1, your decision support tool is sorting on total scores. (Recall that total refers to the values returned for each country from your weighted model calculations). In the previous chapter, you sent a command to your backend database table to sort each country by name. Considering the trouble you had in building the formula for the list box that was required to connect to the table, sending a command to sort the table made sense. It was an easy one-line operation.

However, in this case, you want to have the ability to sort on of any of the metrics, not just the total. But it wouldn't make sense to use VBA to sort the table directly as you did with the country names. Every time you change the sort order of the table, you lose the alphabetical order required for the list box on the menu screen. You could develop the capability to automatically sort the list box every time a user activates the menu screen, but why bother? Because you'd then have to do the same for the analysis screen (re-sort by the last option selected by the user). Clearly you need a way to sort on the data references in the backend table without changing its inherent sort order.

■ **Tip** It might help to think about the different sort types conceptually. The backend database is only sorted when you've added or deleted a record. As such, its inherent state is always that of an alphabetical sort order—and you only re-sort when changes to the underlying data are made to the table. On the other hand, here you're doing work *on top of* the data from that database to answer questions and investigate. Therefore, because you're not changing any underlying data, you want to leave the database sort order intact. In fact, it's important you do as little to the underlying data as possible lest you accidentally corrupt it.

Let's take a look at Figure 8-24. The Sort Column Id input cell tells you which column you're sorting. The numbers to the right of the cell are the Id's. For instance, if you're sorting by the total, the number in Sort Column Id is 6, consistent with what's shown in Figure 8-24. If you want to sort on Health Level, Sort Column Id would be 1. The dynamic is fairly intuitive.

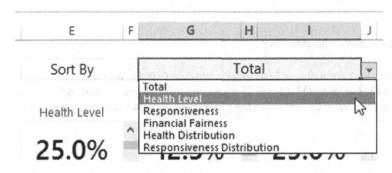

#	Sort Column: Total	Match Index	Country	Health Level	Responsiveness	Financial Fairness	Health Distribution	Responsiveness Distribution	Total

Sort Column Id: 6   1   2   3   4   5   6

Figure 8-24. *The Sort Column Id input cell and Id's corresponding to each metric*

You automatically find the Sort Column Id you're interested in by using the Sort By dropdown box from the visual portion of the tool. Figure 8-25 shows the dropdown from the dashboard.

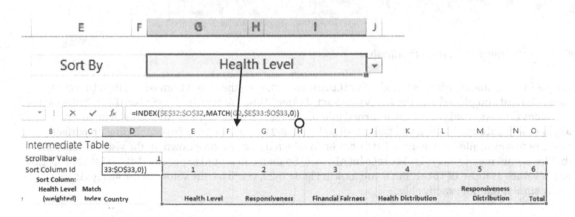

Figure 8-25. *The Sort By dropdown box*

The user response from the Sort By dropdown is used to lookup the correct Column Id, as shown in Figure 8-26.

Figure 8-26. *Health Level from the dropdown is matched to the column names below*

You use the INDEX/MATCH dynamic to help you ultimately find the Id you're interested in. Health Level is matched to its location in the range E33:O33. Because it's in the first cell, Excel returns a 1. You then supply the index that matches its location (in this case, a 1) to the range above and pull out the number given by that matched location. It's like an HLOOKUP, but in reverse.

So let's now jump back to your database. You have this new column that's been added called the Analysis Sort Column.

The Sort Column, Your New Best Friend

In this section, I'll talk about using a sort column to help you sort data from multiple columns. Sort columns are necessary for whenever you want the ability to sort different fields or metrics through the use of a single mechanism. So let's take a look at the formula from the first cell in the Analysis Sort Column in Figure 8-27.

```
Analysis Sort
   Column ▼

=INDEX(Database[@[Health Level (weighted)]:[Total]],
Analysis.SortColumnId)+[@[Country Id]]/10000
```

Figure 8-27. *The first cell in the Analysis Sort Column in the database*

The table expressions inside the INDEX may look confusing at first, so let's only deal with the left-hand side of it for now. The referent Database[@[Health Level (weighted)]:[Total]] is simply a row reference. Figure 8-28 shows the row reference for the first cell. I talked about the Sort Column Id in the previous section, but here you get to see it work its magic.

=INDEX(Database[@[Health Level (weighted)]:[Total]],**Analysis.SortColumnId**)

	I	J	K	L	M	N	
	Health Level (weighted) ▼	Responsiveness (weighted) ▼	Financial Fairness (weighted) ▼	Health Distribution (weighted)▼	Responsiveness Distribution (weighted) ▼	Total ▼	A
0	0.0500	0.0250	0.0250	0.2000	0.1250	42.5	=IN

Figure 8-28. *A selected row from within the database*

Based on the formula above, when Analysis.SortColumnId = 1, then the values from within Health Level (weighted) are returned and placed into the Analysis Sort Column. When Analysis.SortColumnId = 2, the values from within Responsiveness (weighted) are returned into the Analysis Sort Column. And so forth up to Total, which is Analysis.SortColumnId = 6. If you take a look at Figure 8-21, you'll see your Column Id line up perfectly.

For the sake of this example, let's assume Total has been selected from the dropdown on the visual layer of the Analysis tab. This would mean Analysis.ScoreColumnId = 6. So then you should expect the Analysis Sort Column to have the same values as those of Total. But if you look at Figure 8-29, you'll see the values in the Analysis Sort Column are really similar but not exactly alike.

	weights						
	25.00%	12.50%	25.00%	25.00%	12.50%		
▼	Health Level (weighted) ▼	Responsiveness (weighted) ▼	Financial Fairness (weighted) ▼	Health Distribution (weighted) ▼	Responsiveness Distribution (weighted) ▼	Total ▼	Analysis Sort Column ▼
0	0.0500	0.0250	0.0250	0.2000	0.1250	42.5	42.503
3	0.1000	0.0250	0.1000	0.0500	0.0375	31.3	31.252
2	0.1250	0.1125	0.1000	0.2500	0.0250	61.3	61.251
1	0.1250	0.0875	0.1500	0.0250	0.0125	40.0	40.002
8	0.1250	0.1000	0.2250	0.1250	0.1000	67.5	67.504
8	0.0750	0.0125	0.2500	0.0250	0.1000	46.3	46.251
8	0.2250	0.0875	0.1250	0.2250	0.1000	76.3	76.255
3	0.1500	0.1000	0.1750	0.2500	0.0375	71.3	71.252
5	0.2500	0.1125	0.2250	0.2000	0.0625	85.0	85.000

Figure 8-29. *Analysis Sort Column is set to sort on Total values, but notice that they are slightly different than the values in the Total column*

I'll go into why they're slightly off in a moment—and why you *need* them to be slightly off. (Hint, hint: it has to do with the second half of the formula shown in Figure 8-27). But for now, you're going to execute a method called formula-based sorting. With formula-based sorting, you usually use either the LARGE or SMALL functions. Both of these functions work similarly. The prototypes for the LARGE and SMALL functions are

LARGE(array, k) and SMALL(array, k)

In either function, you supply a series of numbers in the first argument. The second argument instructs Excel to return the largest or smallest number in the list. For instance, LARGE(A1:A10, 2) returns the second largest number in the list of numbers stored in cells A1:A10; SMALL(C1:C10, 4) returns the fourth smallest number in the list of numbers stored in cells C1:C10. If you want to use these formulas to return a sorted a list of numbers from greatest to least, you use LARGE and make the K=1 in the first cell; then use LARGE again and make K=2 for the next cell. For each cell, you increment K until it equals the total size of the list.

Let's jump back to the intermediate table. You're now interested in the column with the heading starting with Sort Column:. Figure 8-30 shows the formula for the heading. Note that it's similar to the formula shown in Figure 8-27. However, in that formula, you were interested each row of data. Here, you're instead only in the headers. This formula will always bring up the header of the current metric you're interested in. You won't really use the column header for anything in the visualization layer, but when you have dynamic elements, it always helps to keep track of what you're looking at!

B33	▼	:	×	✓	fx	="Sort Column: " & INDEX(Database[[#Headers],[Health Level (weighted)]:[Total]],Analysis.SortColumnId)

	A	B	C	D	E	F	G	H	I	J	K	L	M
31		Scrollbar Value		1									
32		Sort Column Id		6	1		2		3		4		5
33	#	Sort Column: Total	Match Index Country		Health Level		Responsiveness		Financial Fairness		Health Distribution		Responsivenes Distributioı
34	1	87.5027	14 Foujan		90		90		100		100		3ı

Figure 8-30. *The Sort Column always reflects the current header from within the database of the current column you're interested in sorting on*

Now you use the index list on the left of the Sort Column to return the greatest numbers in the list. Figure 8-31 shows the first cell in the Sort Column. As you can probably guess, when used supply the 1 to the LARGE function, you're returning back the first largest number in the entire column range Database[Analysis Sort Column]. In the second row, you're pulling back the second largest item; in the third row, you're pulling back the third largest item; and so forth. Figure 8-32 shows the formulas for the list.

	#	Sort Column: Total	Match Index	Country
33				
34	1	=LARGE(Database[Analysis Sort Column],A34)		
35	2	86.2533	15	Gaqua
36	3	85.0002	9	Efros
37	4	81.2525	16	Heiestan
38	5	76.2550	7	Ecaislana
39	6	75.0015	17	Hoanga
40	7	73.7548	13	Esnhil
41	8	72.5038	19	Ithha
42	9	71.2519	30	Puodeiton
43	10	71.2516	8	Efbrye
44	11	68.7510	27	Otiaflium
45	12	67.5037	5	Boostan
46	13	65.0013	37	Sodal
47	14	65.0001	22	Muburg
48	15	62.5003	36	Socia
49	16	61.2512	3	Agrines
50	17	60.0036	12	Eqblines
51	18	57.5029	35	Seoceudan
52	19	53.7535	23	Neiestein
53	20	53.7526	39	Urwhary

Figure 8-31. *You use LARGE to create a sorted list from the data stored in the Analysis Sort Column from the database*

#	Sort Column: Total	Match Index Country	Health Level	Respo
1	87.5027	=LARGE(Database[Analysis Sort Column],A34)		
2	86.2533	=LARGE(Database[Analysis Sort Column],A35)		
3	85.0002	=LARGE(Database[Analysis Sort Column],A36)		
4	81.2525	=LARGE(Database[Analysis Sort Column],A37)		
5	76.2550	=LARGE(Database[Analysis Sort Column],A38)		
6	75.0015	=LARGE(Database[Analysis Sort Column],A39)		
7	73.7548	=LARGE(Database[Analysis Sort Column],A40)		
8	72.5038	=LARGE(Database[Analysis Sort Column],A41)		
9	71.2519	=LARGE(Database[Analysis Sort Column],A42)		
10	71.2516	=LARGE(Database[Analysis Sort Column],A43)		
11	68.7510	=LARGE(Database[Analysis Sort Column],A44)		
12	67.5037	=LARGE(Database[Analysis Sort Column],A45)		
13	65.0013	=LARGE(Database[Analysis Sort Column],A46)		
14	65.0001	=LARGE(Database[Analysis Sort Column],A47)		
15	62.5003	=LARGE(Database[Analysis Sort Column],A48)		
16	61.2512	=LARGE(Database[Analysis Sort Column],A49)		
17	60.0036	=LARGE(Database[Analysis Sort Column],A50)		
18	57.5029	=LARGE(Database[Analysis Sort Column],A51)		
19	53.7535	=LARGE(Database[Analysis Sort Column],A52)		
20	53.7526	=LARGE(Database[Analysis Sort Column],A53)		

Is Sorted On?   FALSE

Figure 8-32. *The formulas return a sorted list*

The Match Index Column, the Sort Column's Buddy

You now have a sorted list of data. But the obvious question is to which country do these data points belong? Having a list of sorted data tells you little if anything by itself. So now you'll need to build a Match Index (again, this follows the simple example from Chapter 6). The Match Index simply tells you the index location of where your sorted data points are located back in your database.

Figure 8-33 shows the formula you use in the Match Index column. You simply match the adjacent value back into the Analysis Sort Column. It's important to remember the Analysis Sort Column *isn't* sorted. Therefore, the largest values are likely to be all over the place. As you see from Figure 8-33, the second largest value is in the 15th row, the third in the 9th row, etc.

| ACOT | ▼ | : | ✕ | ✓ | fx | =MATCH(B34,Database[Analysis Sort Column],0) |

	A	B	C	D	E	F	G	H
		Sort Column:	Match					
33	#	Total	Index	Country	Health Level		Responsiveness	
34	1	87.5027	=MATCH	Foujan	90		90	
35	2	86.2533	15	Gaqua	80		50	
36	3	85.0002	9	Efros	100		90	
37	4	81.2525	16	Heiestan	70		50	
38	5	76.2550	7	Ecaislana	90		70	
39	6	75.0015	17	Hoanga	50		90	
40	7	73.7548	13	Esnhil	80		100	
41	8	72.5038	19	Ithha	100		10	
42	9	71.2519	30	Puodeiton	70		70	
43	10	71.2516	8	Efbrye	60		80	
44	11	68.7510	27	Otiaflium	100		30	
45	12	67.5037	5	Boostan	50		80	
46	13	65.0013	37	Sodal	70		50	
47	14	65.0001	22	Muburg	90		10	
48	15	62.5003	36	Socia	40		30	
49	16	61.2512	3	Agrines	50		90	
50	17	60.0036	12	Eqblines	40		20	
51	18	57.5029	35	Seoceudan	10		40	
52	19	53.7535	23	Neiestein	80		30	
53	20	53.7526	39	Urwhary	70		40	

Figure 8-33. *The Match Index shows the index location each sorted value can be found back in its original column*

And once you know the row location of where the total value has been matched, you can use that information to look up the country name. Figure 8-34 shows the formula you use to look up the country name.

	A	B	C	D	E	F
		Sort Column:	Match			
33	#	Total	Index	Country	Health Level	
34	1	87.5027	14	=INDEX(Database[Country Name],C34)		
35	2	86.2533	15	Gaqua	80	
36	3	85.0002	9	Efros	100	
37	4	81.2525	16	Heiestan	70	
38	5	76.2550	7	Ecaislana	90	
39	6	75.0015	17	Hoanga	50	

Figure 8-34. *You simply use the Match Index to find the row location of the data you're interested in*

And you can do the same with Health Level (Figure 8-35), Responsiveness, Financial Fairness, Health Distribution, Responsiveness Distribution, and the Total. Everything displayed on the intermediate table uses the Match Index column.

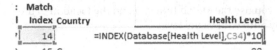

: Match I Index	Country	Health Level
14		=INDEX(Database[Health Level],C34)*10

Figure 8-35. *Using the Match Index to find the current Health Level*

You Have a "Unique" Problem

Using MATCH to look through the Analysis Sort Column works terrifically, assuming you have no duplicate values. Remember, MATCH will always return the index of only the first instance of the matched item in a list. (MATCH does not really care if there are other items in the list once it's found the value it's searching for.)

In Figure 8-36, notice that some total values do indeed repeat. In your ranking, they essentially form a tie. However, unless you do something, MATCH will always find that first 41.3 and return that row location. So you need some way to differentiate the first instance of 41.3 from all the instances that follow. And you do that by creating some noise in the data.

8	Country Id	Country Name	Responsiveness Distribution (weighted)	Total
36	21	Pocor	0.0250	41.3
37	39	Puafoabia	0.0250	43.8
38	19	Puodeiton	0.0250	71.3
39	41	Pustein	0.0750	46.3
40	31	Rana	0.0750	51.3
41	7	Sauolia	0.1125	41.3

Figure 8-36. *Pocor and Sauolia have the same score*

Remember the second half of the formula in Figure 8-37? Let's see it action (Figure 8-37).

	A	B	M	N	O	P	Q	R
8	Country Id	Country Name	Responsiveness Distribution (weighted)	Total	Analysis Sort Column			
9	30	Acoaslesh	0.1250	42.5	=INDEX(Database[@[Health Level (weighted)]:			
10	24	Afon	0.0375	31.3	[Total]],Analysis.SortColumnId)+[@[Country			
11	12	Agrines	0.0250	61.3	Id]]/10000			

Figure 8-37. *Focus on the second half of the Analysis Sort Column formula*

The second half of that formula, [@[County Id]]/10000, simply adds an incredibly small amount to data returned by INDEX function in the left-hand side of the formula. In Figure 8-37, you're adding the amount 30/10000. Since Country Id is always unique, you can be assured that even when you have totals that aren't unique, once you add this small amount *the results will always be unique*.

And remember, you only use the Analysis Sort Column from the database to help you find the locations of certain rows. That is, it helps you find the Match Index. From there, you use the Match Index to find the location of the information you're interested in. The noisy data never makes its way onto your visual layer.

Seeing It Work Altogether

The scrolling and sorting mechanisms are now complete. In fact, you can see them working together. If you adjust the scroll bar from in the visual layer, you'll see the intermediate table change. Figure 8-38 shows the scroll bar at value 19.

	#	Sort Column: Total	Match Index	Country	Health Level	Responsiveness	Financial Fairness	Health Distribution	Responsiveness Distribution	Total
30		Intermediate Table								
31		Scrollbar Value		19						
32		Sort Column Id		6	1	2	3	4	5	6
33										
34	19	53.7535	23	Neiestein	80	30	20	50	100	53.75
35	20	53.7526	39	Urwhary	70	40	50	60	30	53.75
36	21	52.5020	18	Iqeiskya	60	20	50	60	60	52.50
37	22	51.2531	32	Rana	20	30	70	70	60	51.25
38	23	46.2541	31	Pustein	10	30	70	60	60	46.25
39	24	46.2509	6	Dovaeria	30	10	100	10	80	46.25
40	25	45.0014	25	Opium	40	90	40	50	10	45.00
41	26	43.7539	29	Puafoabia	30	10	90	40	20	43.75
42	27	42.5032	24	Obron	10	80	50	20	100	42.50
43	28	42.5030	1	Acoaslesh	20	20	10	80	100	42.50
44	29	42.5028	11	Eprvil	20	80	60	20	60	42.50
45	30	41.2521	28	Pocor	50	30	70	20	20	41.25
46	31	41.2507	33	Sauolia	40	80	30	10	90	41.25
47	32	40.0022	4	Asnon	50	70	60	10	10	40.00
48	33	38.7551	38	Stansblink	20	30	40	50	60	38.75
49	34	36.2506	10	Elsmen	30	10	20	80	20	36.25
50	35	35.0052	21	Jordan	40	50	20	30	50	35.00
51	36	31.2524	2	Afon	40	20	40	20	30	31.25
52	37	31.2511	20	Jaca	90	20	10	10	10	31.25
53	38	30.0008	26	Osppar	30	60	20	10	60	30.00
54				Is Sorted On?	FALSE	FALSE	FALSE	FALSE	FALSE	TRUE

Figure 8-38. *Notice that the index now starts with 19*

Notice your table now shows the country ranked in the 19th place in terms of its overall total score. Figure 8-39 shows what happens when you change the Sort By to Responsiveness.

	#	Sort Column: Responsiveness (weighted)	Match Index	Country	Health Level	Responsiveness	Financial Fairness	Health Distribution	Responsiveness Distribution	Total
					1	2	3	4	5	6
34	19	0.0650	16	Heiestan	70	50	80	100	100	81.25
35	20	0.0638	37	Sodal	70	50	30	100	70	65.00
36	21	0.0529	35	Seoceudan	10	40	90	90	40	57.50
37	22	0.0526	39	Urwhary	70	40	50	60	30	53.75
38	23	0.0426	38	Stansblink	20	30	40	50	60	38.75
39	24	0.0416	31	Pustein	10	30	70	60	60	46.25
40	25	0.0410	23	Neiestein	80	30	20	50	100	53.75
41	26	0.0406	32	Rana	20	30	70	70	60	51.25
42	27	0.0396	28	Pocor	50	30	70	20	20	41.25
43	28	0.0385	27	Otiaflium	100	30	60	90	20	68.75
44	29	0.0378	36	Socla	40	30	100	70	50	62.50
45	30	0.0286	12	Fqhlines	40	20	90	90	20	60.00
46	31	0.0280	1	Acoaslesh	20	20	10	80	100	42.50
47	32	0.0274	2	Afon	40	20	40	20	30	31.25
48	33	0.0270	18	Iqeiskya	60	20	50	60	60	52.50
49	34	0.0261	20	Jaca	90	20	10	10	10	31.25
50	35	0.0164	29	Puafoabia	30	10	90	40	20	43.75
51	36	0.0163	19	Ithha	100	10	90	70	50	72.50
52	37	0.0134	6	Dovaeria	30	10	100	10	80	46.25
53	38	0.0131	10	Eismen	30	10	20	80	20	36.25
54		Is Sorted On?			FALSE	TRUE	FALSE	FALSE	FALSE	FALSE

Above the table: Intermediate Table; Scrollbar Value 19; Sort Column Id 2.

Figure 8-39. *Responsivness is now the sort factor*

Notice that the Sort Column Id now shows the number 2, reflecting the column you're interested in sorting on. And the Sort Column shows that you are sorting on Responsiveness (weighted). Your intermediate table now has a different sort order than you had previously when you were sorting on the Total; however, you've made no changes to the underlying data.

The Last Word

In this chapter, I talked about the type of analysis you will be performing on your data. You created the infrastructure to easily apply one-way sensitivity analysis. Further, you used formulas to create a robust sorting mechanism that can sort more than one type of metric. Finally, you used the form control Scroll Bar so you don't have to show all the data all at once. This work builds on what's been completed in previous chapters.

In the next chapter, you'll build the visual layer in full.

■ ■ ■

CHAPTER 9

Perfecting the Presentation

In the previous chapter, you learned to build the intermediate table, which deals largely with transforming the raw data from the backend database. The presentation or visual layer, on the other hand, deals largely with what the user sees.

In this chapter, you'll focus on the visual layer as well as its interaction with the intermediate table. Just as before, the focus here is to create a lightweight infrastructure that isn't heavily steeped in code. You'll be using the file Chapter9Wizard.xlsm for this chapter. I recommend having it open as you follow along.

Implementation and Design of the Weight Adjustment System

In this section, I'll talk about implementing the weight adjustment system, shown in Figure 9-1. You'll find this across the top of your Analysis screen.

Figure 9-1. *The weight adjustment system*

Each box is simply connected to the associated weight on the Helper tab. Figure 9-2 shows the connection to Health Level. Note that each metric follows suit.

Figure 9-2. *Each weight box is connected directly to the associated weights from on the Helper tab*

Likewise, the scroll bars here are exactly like the ones on the Helper tab you built in the previous chapter (Figure 9-3). However, I don't recommend copying and pasting those scroll bars from the Helper tab and placing them on this tab. Scroll bars are usually set to relative references. If you copy and paste the scroll bars from the Helper tab, Excel will try to change the same cell address on the Analysis tab. That's not what you want.

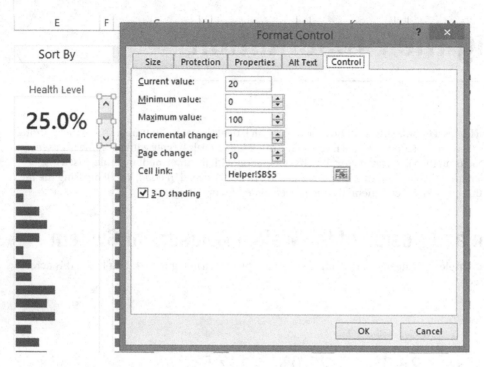

Figure 9-3. *Properties for the scroll bar. Notice the cell link is the same as that of the scroll bars on the Helper tab*

Your best bet is to insert each of these scroll bars manually. In Figure 9-4, you can see that I've left some space in Column F between each weight box to provide a place for a scroll bar. I used a similar space between all the weight boxes. This is similar to the process of *anchoring* described in Chapter 7.

The scroll bar sits atop this buffer in column F.

Figure 9-4. *I've moved the scroll bar to the side to show the column spacer*

Next, enable the Snap to Grid feature by right-clicking or Ctrl+clicking the scroll bar. From the Format context tab, pick Align and select Snap To Grid (see Figure 9-5).

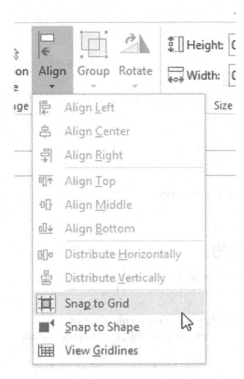

Figure 9-5. *The Snap To Grid feature*

The Snap to Grid feature will force you to align Excel's cell grid. So if you size a spacer column as I did in Figure 9-4 in Column F, ensuring consistent alignment and size for each scroll bar is easy peasy. Of course, the "correct" size is more art than science. To make my life easier, I like to design the first scroll bar spacer. Once I like the size, I right-click the column and select column width to find out its size (Figure 9-6).

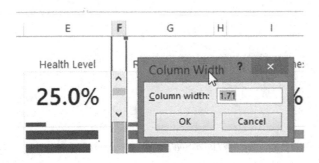

Figure 9-6. *Column width for column F*

Then I right-click every other similar column and set its size to be the same. As you can see in Figure 9-7, 1.71 is what I liked best, but you may differ. As you may have guessed, I did the same for the weight boxes.

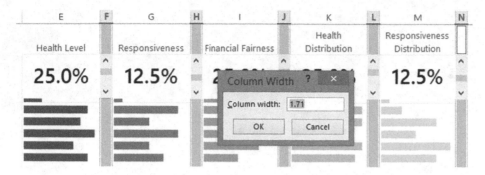

Figure 9-7. *Selecting similar columns and setting their size all at once to ensure consistency*

Displaying Data from the Intermediate Table

Now let's talk about how to display data from the intermediate table. For the most part, it's a one-to-one mapping. That is, if you look at Health Level in the visual presentation, you can scroll down to see the data it is visualizing directly underneath. They share the same column.

The are a few exceptions to this. Ideally, it would be great if all data items shared the same columns but sometimes the way your data is laid out constrains this ideal. (Of course, as you can see from this, I always try to align them as much as possible.) So let's go through each item in the visual layer.

Results Information Label

This section talks about building the results information formula. Figure 9-8 shows the results of this formula. The "7-26 of 39" means the results ranked from 7 to 26 are currently in view, out of 39 total possible items available. The formula updates as the scroll bar changes (Figure 9-9).

Figure 9-8. *The results information label shows the ranked items currently in view as well as the final total of items*

The formula uses the first ranked item in the list and the last ranked item in the list to define the range of numbers in view. Database.RecordCount is used to show the total amount of records available for view (Figure 9-9).

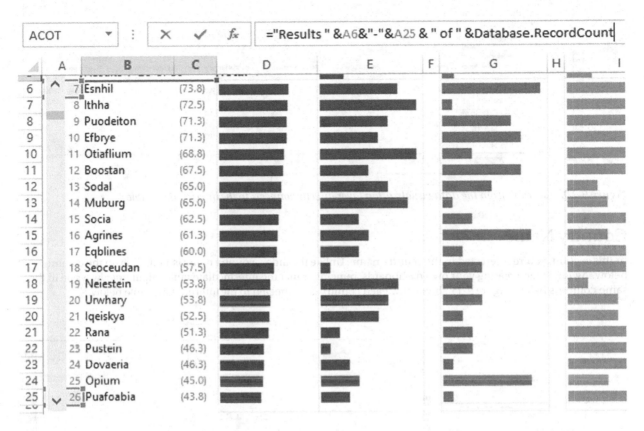

Figure 9-9. The results information label formula

The Current Rank of Each Country

The first item on the left is the current rank of each country shown. This value is pulled directly from the index created in the intermediate table. Figure 9-10 shows how the rank and index connect.

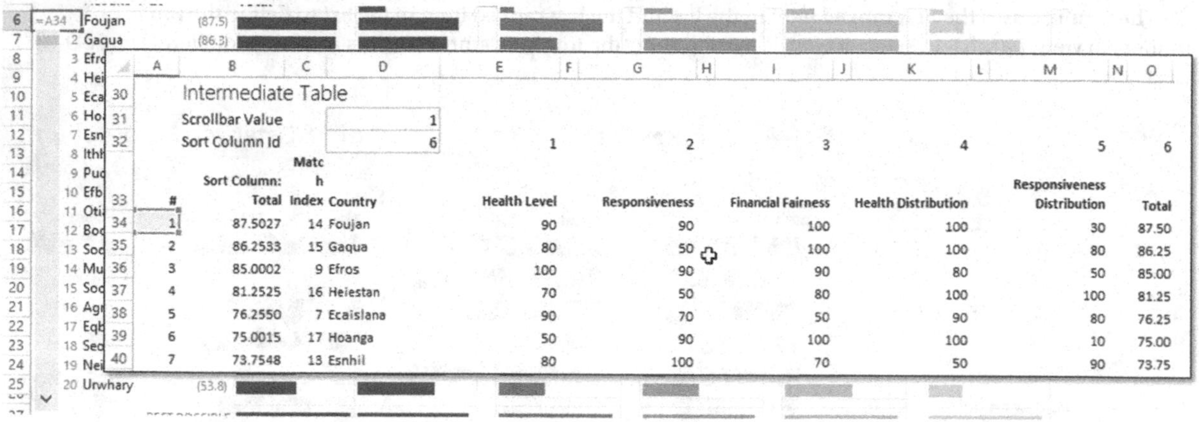

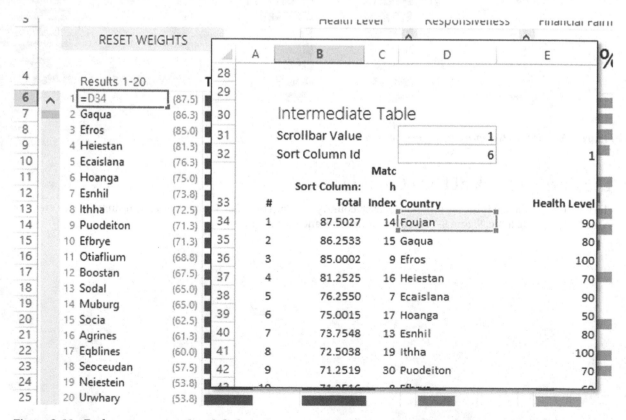

Figure 9-10. *The rank from the data visualization layer directly connects to the intermediate table*

Country Name

In this section, you're interested in the country name. Unlike the index, country name isn't directly in the column below. Again, when creating your own dashboards, remember that the intermediate table might not always be in the same columns below. Figure 9-11 shows how each country is connected to the intermediate table below.

Figure 9-11. *Each country name directly links to the intermediate table below, but it's not in the same column*

Total Scores for Each Country

This section will show you how to display the total scores for each country. Recall that the column representing total scores is actually the last column on the right in the intermediate table. Note how this is different for your visual layer. Figure 9-12 shows the connection.

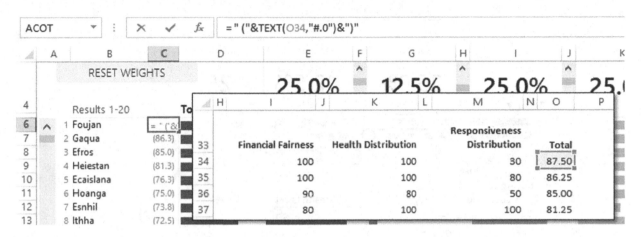

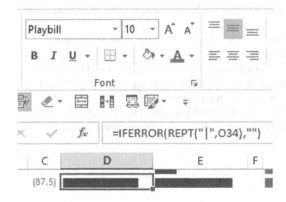

Figure 9-12. *The Total score is one of the first columns in the visual layer and one of the last columns in the intermediate table*

Let's take a moment to look at the formula. I place parentheses around the total value as a means to downplay its importance somewhat. (I'll go over why near the end of the chapter.) Since I'm using the values in the Total cell in a formula, I risk showing more decimal precision than required. Using the TEXT function, I've supplied a formatting rule to ensure you also see everything to the right of the decimal and always one number to the right.

In-cell Bar Charts for All Metrics

The rest of the data items in your visual layer are in-cell bar charts. You can re-create small bar charts using the REPT function and the pipe symbol. Figure 9-13 shows the formula as well as the best font selection for this type of chart. As Figure 9-13 shows, Playbill size 10 is fairly reliable. Notice the cell it refers to is O34. This is the same cell referenced to get the Total value in Figure 9-9.

Figure 9-13. *In-cell bar chart for Total*

Figure 9-14 shows the connection for Health Level. It's virtually the same function setup as that used for Total. In this case, it refers to the Health Level metric from the intermediate table.

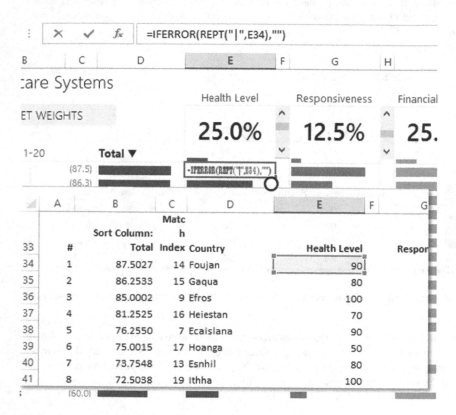

Figure 9-14. *Formula for in-cell bar charts for metric data*

The in-cell bar charts for the rest of the metrics follow suit. Responsiveness, Financial Fairness, Health Distribution, and Responsiveness Distribution all use the REPT function and link to their corresponding column from the intermediate table.

You may be wondering what's going on with that IFERROR. Why does it appear in the function? The answer is because you need it. For one, you won't always have at least 20 entries. If there are less than 20 entries, then you need these cells to appear blank.

More importantly, however, is that you simply don't know what lies ahead. You are using a rather simple example here, so you're unlikely to see any other types of errors. But that's also shortsighted thinking. For example, in my original formulation of this spreadsheet, when you reduced a weight to zero, the result was a #DIV/0 in that metric's column. I didn't want the #DIV/0 error to show when the result should show nothing. Therefore, I used the IFERROR function as shown above. While subsequent changes to the model make such an error unlikely, I've kept it in just in case. However, I'm unconvinced that daring folks out there can't figure out a way to create errors I couldn't foresee. Moreover, since the proliferation of errors in cells can seriously slow down a spreadsheet, preventing them is important.

Best Possible Comparisons

At the bottom of the of the visual layer I've included the best possible scores for each metric. This allows the user to compare instantly the results against the best result. Since 100 is the best possible score, the formula for each of these cells is always =REPT("|", 100) (see Figure 9-15).

Figure 9-15. *The formula for best possible comparisons*

Weight Box Progress Meters

Under each weight box is a progress meter that shows works exactly like the in-cell bar charts. In the Figure 9-16, you can see each small bar chart within a weight box.

Figure 9-16. *The small lines under each weight box are progress meters*

Figure 9-17 shows the formula used for these bar charts. Notice the theme here. It's essentially the same formula. However, to make it appear smaller, I've just resized the row.

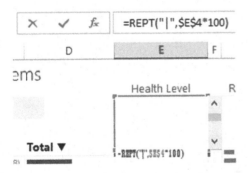

Figure 9-17. *The progress bars under each weight value are minified versions of the same bar chart formula used previously*

"Sort By" Dropdown and Sort Labels

In the last chapter, you built the infrastructure for sorting. In this section, I'll talk about the visual elements that go along with that sorting mechanic. One of the cool features of your sorting system is that you can use the Sort By dropdown to select which metric you'd like to sort by. Once the user has made their selection, the corresponding column label becomes bold and the down arrow appears next to it (see Figure 9-18).

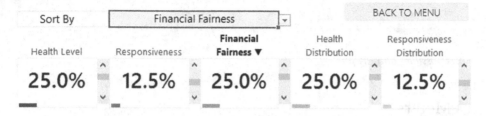

Figure 9-18. *The Financial Fairness label becomes bold and a down arrow appears next to it*

Following the no-code theme, this mechanism requires no VBA. However, it is a mixture of several different elements, which I'll go through in the next few sections.

Dropdown Metric Selection

In this section, I'll talk about the Sort By dropdown. It's nothing more than a data validation list (Figure 9-19), which you can insert into the spreadsheet from the Data tab. Generally, I don't like to type the list source in directly. However, the areas in which these selections appear on the spreadsheet do not appear in one contiguous region. If you look at your current sheet, you'll see that you don't have one list of data where Total, Health Level, etc. appear without any cells in between. If you were to link directly to these sources, there would be space in your dropdowns. So typing the text in directly here works best even if it's not preferred.

Figure 9-19. *The Data Validation dialog box showing the dropdown list you've created*

Using Boolean Formulas to Define Which Metric Has Been Selected

Recall from the previous section that changes in the dropdown change the Sort Column Id. Since you selected Financial Fairness in Figure 9-19, the Sort Column Id is a 3, as expected (Figure 9-20).

				1	2	3	4	5	6
30	Intermediate Table								
31	Scrollbar Value		7						
32	Sort Column Id		3						
33	#	Financial Fairness (weighted)	Match Index Country	Health Level	Responsiveness	Financial Fairness	Health Distribution	Responsiveness Distribution	Total
34	7	0.2289	29 Puafoabia	30	10	90	40	20	43.75
35	8	0.2288	19 Ithha	100	10	90	70	50	72.50
36	9	0.2287	5 Boostan	50	80	90	50	80	67.50
37	10	0.2286	12 Eqblines	40	20	90	90	20	60.00
38	11	0.2279	35 Seoceudan	10	40	90	90	40	57.50
39	12	0.2252	9 Efros	100	90	90	80	50	85.00
40	13	0.2025	16 Heiestan	70	50	80	100	100	81.25
41	14	0.1798	13 Esnhil	80	100	70	50	90	73.75
42	15	0.1791	31 Pustein	10	30	70	60	60	46.25
43	16	0.1781	32 Rana	20	30	70	70	60	51.25
44	17	0.1771	28 Pocor	50	30	70	20	20	41.25
45	18	0.1766	8 Efbrye	60	80	70	100	30	71.25
46	19	0.1528	11 Eprvil	20	80	60	20	60	42.50
47	20	0.1522	4 Asnon	50	70	60	10	10	40.00
48	21	0.1510	27 Otiaflium	100	30	60	90	20	68.75
49	22	0.1300	7 Ecaislana	90	70	50	90	80	76.25
50	23	0.1282	24 Obron	10	80	50	20	100	42.50
51	24	0.1276	39 Urwhary	70	40	50	60	30	53.75
52	25	0.1270	18 Iqeiskya	60	20	50	60	60	52.50
53	26	0.1051	88 Stansblink	20	30	40	50	60	38.75
54		Is Sorted On?		FALSE	FALSE	TRUE	FALSE	FALSE	FALSE

Figure 9-20. Sort Column Id is equal to 3

At the bottom of Figure 9-20 is a line item that reads, "Is Sorted On?" This row highlights the row currently being sorted on. Notice for all columns except for Financial Fairness, the value reads FALSE. For Financial Fairness, the value reads TRUE. This is because you're sorting on this metric. Figure 9-21 shows the formula you're using in this row.

Intermediate Table

Scrollbar Value		7		
Sort Column Id		3	1	2
Financial Fairness (weighted)	Match Index	Country	Health Level	Responsiveness
0.2289	29	Puafoabia	30	10
0.2288	19	Ithha	100	10
0.2287	5	Boostan	50	80
0.2286	12	Eqblines	40	20
0.2279	35	Seoceudan	10	40
0.2252	9	Efros	100	90
0.2025	16	Heiestan	70	50
0.1798	13	Esnhil	80	100
0.1791	31	Pustein	10	30
0.1781	32	Rana	20	30
0.1771	28	Pocor	50	30
0.1766	8	Efbrye	60	80
0.1528	11	Eprvil	20	80
0.1522	4	Asnon	50	70
0.1510	27	Otiaflium	100	30
0.1300	7	Ecaislana	90	70
0.1282	24	Obron	10	80
0.1276	39	Urwhary	70	40
0.1270	18	Iqeiskya	60	20
0.1051	38	Stansblink	20	30
		Is Sorted On?	FALSE	=(G32=$D$32)

Figure 9-21. *The Boolean formula used to test whether you're sorting on a specific column*

You'll use this Boolean formula to perform conditional formatting and add the down arrow to each header.

Connecting Everything with Conditional Format Highlighting

In this section, you'll put the finishing touches on each header by conditionally formatting the selected column header as bold. This should hopefully feel somewhat familiar to you as it's a reapplication of the Highlight mechanism described in Chapter 4. (Remember, if you think of it as a reusable component, you can apply it to many different spreadsheet applications.) Figure 9-22 shows the Conditional Formatting Rules Manager for cells E3:M3. Notice I've applied conditional formatting rules to these column headers. You can see it for yourself by selecting cells E3:M3, clicking on the Conditional Formatting dropdown box from the Home tab, and selecting Manage Rules.

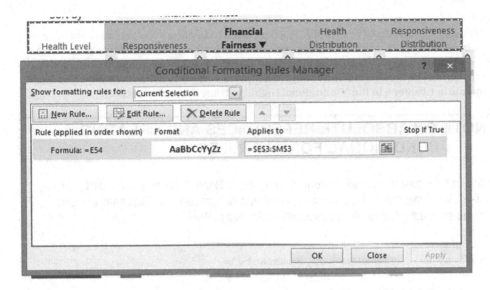

Figure 9-22. *The Conditional Formatting Rules Manager dialog box*

Let's take a look at the conditional formatting rules behind the scenes. If you click on Edit Rule, you will see the Edit Formatting Rule dialog box (Figure 9-23).

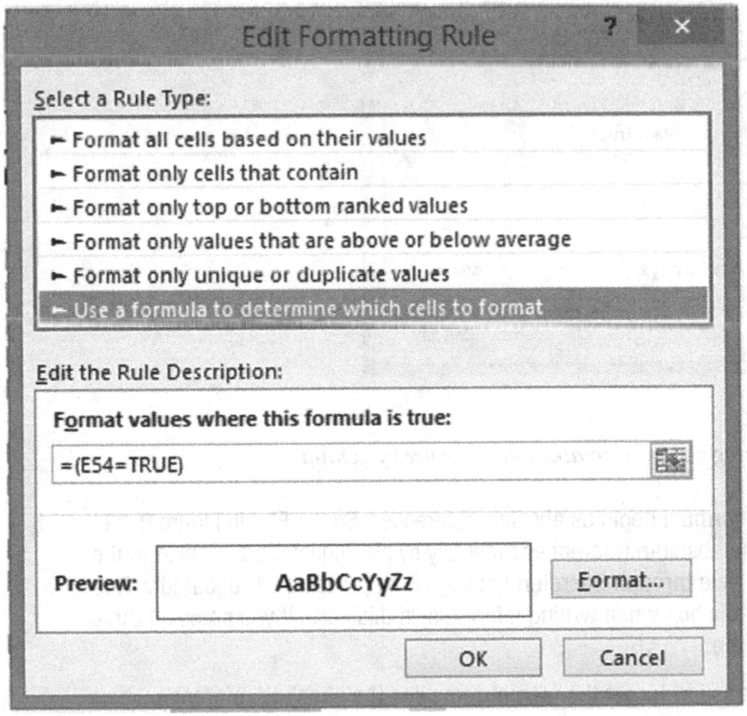

Figure 9-23. *The Edit Formatting Rule dialog box*

Note that I've selected "Use a formula to determine which cells to format." In the "Format values where this formula is true" rule type, I'm using the formula =(E54=TRUE). This formula is what allows you to change the style of font of the sort column that's been selected. In addition, notice that I'm not using the absolute cell reference $E$54. That absolute cell reference is what appears by default. However, if you kept the absolute reference, it would only test cell E54. Instead, you want the test for conditional formatting to happen across every cell in the range. You might recall you built a similar dynamic in Chapter 4 in the "Conditional Highlight Using Formulas" section.

A QUICK NOTE ON ABSOLUTE REFERENCES AND CREATING CONDITIONAL FORMAT RULES

If you select "Use a formula to determine which cells to format" as I have in Figure 9-23, you won't start with relative references by default. What that means is, if you were to set up this formula for the first time, and you selected cell E54 from on the spreadsheet, it would look something like Figure 9-24.

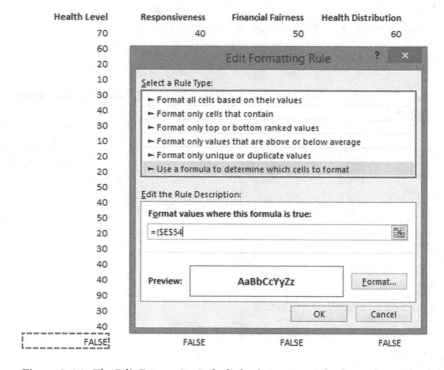

Figure 9-24. *The Edit Formatting Rule dialog box uses an absolute reference by default*

By default, all cells selected to populate the formula begin as absolute references. So the E54 in Figure 9-23 actually began as E54. You can change the absolute references manually by placing your cursor next to the dollar signs and deleting them. Or, you can cycle through the references types by pressing F4 repeatedly. This is similar to pressing F4 repeatedly in the formula box when writing a formula. In this case, if you press F4 three times, you'll arrive at the relative cell reference.

When you first set the cell, it's sometimes easy to forget the step of removing the absolute reference when it's necessary.

If you click the Format button (see Figure 9-24), you'll be taken to the Format Cells dialog box. Here, you can change the format of the cells whose sort column has been selected. For my formatting choices, I've selected a Bold font style (Figure 9-25). I've stayed away from doing any other embellishments. You don't want the selected header to take away from the data visualization portion. Nor do you want it to overwhelm the visual field. If you're not careful, you can go crazy with the formatting options. Here I am being subtle and tasteful.

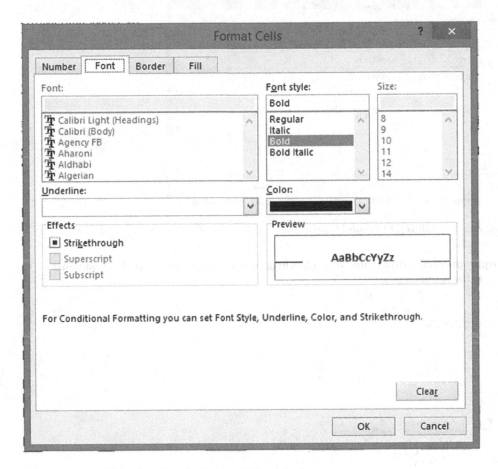

Figure 9-25. *Bold is selected in the Format Cells dialog box*

This conditional formatting rule simply takes care of the metrics across the top. It doesn't take care of Total, which is not part of the same row. So you'll need to make an additional rule just for the total. Remember, however, what the Total row refers to is in a different column on the intermediate table. Take note in Figure 9-26: the rule is set to test the cell in O45, which, unlike the other columns in the visual layer, is not directly below the Total on the intermediate table.

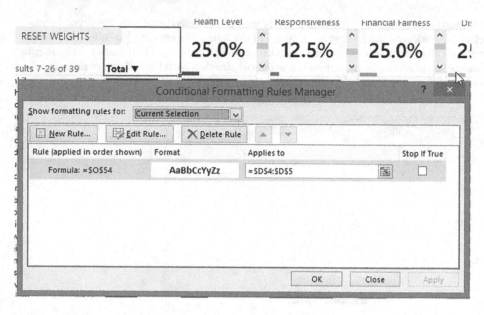

Figure 9-26. *An individual rule is required for the Total header*

The mechanism to display the down arrow in the weight box headings uses the same row as the conditional formatting. Let's take a look at the formulas (Figure 9-27).

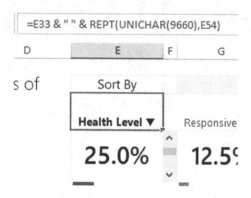

Figure 9-27. *The formula used for the weight box heading*

The left-side of the formula, E33, simply refers to the column header from the intermediate table. But turn your attention to the right side. The down arrow is given by the Unicode index number 9660. And we can display the character with the UNICHAR function. REPT, as you might recall, lets you specify a character in the first argument and the amount of times to repeat that character in the second argument. Here, you've specified that you want to repeat the down arrow. E54 in the formula (the value of how many times you want to repeat the formula) points to TRUE and FALSE. And, if you remember how Boolean functions work, TRUE = 1 and FALSE = 0. So each header uses this formula. When the Is Sorted On row returns TRUE for the corresponding column, it displays the down arrow (it's being repeated 1 time).

The Presentation Display Buttons

In this section, I'll talk about the display buttons available to the user. The first takes the user back to the menu, and the other resets the weights back to the original schema. Figure 9-28 shows these buttons placed adjacent to one another. Your buttons in this case are nothing more than TextBox shapes with macros assigned to execute when the user clicks one.

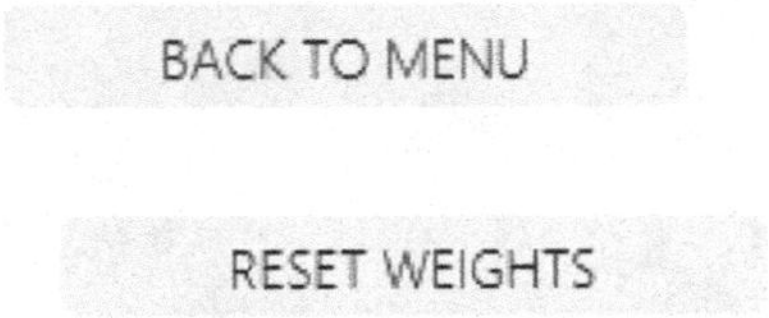

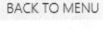

BACK TO MENU

RESET WEIGHTS

Figure 9-28. *The two buttons on your dashboard*

Going Back to the Menu

The Back To Menu button is simple. It simply takes the user back to the Menu screen. It can be found in the sheet object of the Analysis worksheet tab. Listing 9-1 shows all the code that's required.

Listing 9-1. The BackToMenu Procedure

```
Public Sub BackToMenu()
    Welcome.Activate
End Sub
```

Resetting the Weights

Because you're performing sensitivity analysis, you expect the weights to change from their original scheme. Once you've changed the weights, you might find you want to reset them back to the original scheme. Remember what dictates the weights are the ratios of the values of the scroll bars. So, one way to create this weight scheme is with the scroll bar linked value ratios shown in Figure 9-29 from the Helper tab.

	Metrics	Linked Value	Adjusted Value	Final Weight
4				
5	Health Level	20	80	25.0%
6	Responsiveness	60	40	12.5%
7	Financial Fairness	20	80	25.0%
8	Health Distribution	20	80	25.0%
9	Responsiveness Distribution	60	40	12.5%
10	Total		320	100%

Figure 9-29. *The Linked Value column shows the required scroll bar values to get to the original weights*

Below this table on the Helper tab is a column of data that says Saved Weights (Figure 9-30). Notice the values match the exact values in the Linked Value column in Figure 9-29. I've named this column of data as Helper.SavedWeights. Likewise, I've named the column of linked values in Figure 9-29 as Helper.LinkedValues.

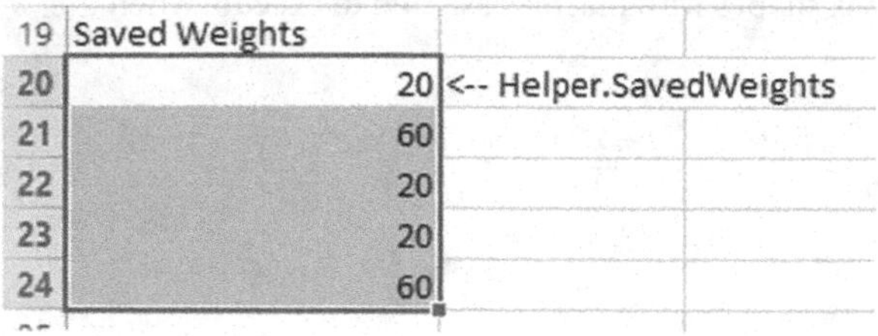

Figure 9-30. *The scroll bar values that help you get to the correct weights*

The Reset Button simply copies these saved values onto the linked values. Listing 9-2 shows the code, which can be found in your file in the Analysis worksheet tab.

Listing 9-2. The ResetWeights Procedure

```
Public Sub ResetWeights()
    [Helper.LinkedValues].Value = [Helper.SavedWeights].Value
End Sub
```

Think about this dynamic for a moment. Here you've saved only schema of weights. But you could save as many weight scenarios as you'd like. It wouldn't be hard to extend this model to have the user save a weight scheme they like. Then later they could load the schema. All you would need is the simple code above to start.

Data Display and Aesthetics

In this section, I'll focus a little bit on the nature of the data you're displaying. In addition, I'll talk about some of the aesthetic choices, including color and spacing. You may have noticed that the nature of the Total data (column O in Figure 9-31) is different than that of the metrics (columns E, G, I, K, and M in Figure 9-31). Specifically, the metric data is all whole multiples of ten from 0 to 100, while the Total data can be any number from 0 to 100.

	A	B	C	D	E	F	G	H	I	J	K	L	M	N O
30		Intermediate Table												
31		Scrollbar Value		20										
32		Sort Column Id		6		1		2		3		4		5 6

33	#	Sort Column: Total	Match Index	Country	Health Level	Responsiveness	Financial Fairness	Health Distribution	Responsiveness Distribution	Total
34	20	53.7526	39	Urwhary	70	40	50	60	30	53.75
35	21	52.5020	18	Iqeiskya	60	20	50	60	60	52.50
36	22	51.2531	32	Rana	20	30	70	70	60	51.25
37	23	46.2541	31	Pustein	10	30	70	60	60	46.25
38	24	46.2509	6	Dovaeria	30	10	100	10	80	46.25
39	25	45.0014	25	Opium	40	90	40	50	10	45.00
40	26	43.7539	29	Puafoabia	30	10	90	40	20	43.75
41	27	42.5032	24	Obron	10	80	50	20	100	42.50
42	28	42.5030	1	Acoaslesh	20	20	10	80	100	42.50
43	29	42.5028	11	Eprvil	20	80	60	20	60	42.50
44	30	41.2521	28	Pocor	50	30	70	20	20	41.25
45	31	41.2507	33	Sauolia	40	80	30	10	90	41.25
46	32	40.0022	4	Asnon	50	70	60	10	10	40.00
47	33	38.7551	38	Stansblink	20	30	40	50	60	38.75
48	34	36.2506	10	Eismen	30	10	20	80	20	36.25
49	35	35.0052	21	Jordan	40	50	20	30	50	35.00
50	36	31.2524	2	Afon	40	20	40	20	30	31.25
51	37	31.2511	20	Jaca	90	20	10	10	10	31.25
52	38	30.0008	26	Osppar	30	60	20	10	60	30.00
53	39	27.5023	34	Segro	40	70	10	10	30	27.50
54		Is Sorted On?			FALSE	FALSE	FALSE	FALSE	FALSE	TRUE

Figure 9-31. The intermediate table shows that the nature of the metric data differs from the total column

Weighted vs. Not-Weighted Metrics

The reason the nature of the Total data is different from the metrics data is that the Total data is *weighted* whereas the metric data is not (Figure 9-32). Responsiveness Distribution, for example, simply uses the formula =INDEX(Database[Health Distribution],C34)*10 in its first row cell, where C34 is the Match Index. Note Database[Health Distribution] isn't a weighted column. You might be wondering why you display the weighted Total but do not display the weighted metrics (note, however, you do use the weighted metrics for your sort even if you don't display the results). I'll talk about that in this section.

5	6
Responsiveness Distribution	Total
70	65.00
90	73.75
100	53.75
80	86.25
30	53.75
100	81.25

Figure 9-32. You display the weighted Total but not weighted metrics

The answer is that displaying the weighted metrics wouldn't do well to highlight the variances between metrics for a single country nor within one metric across several countries. Figure 9-33 shows how the data visualization changes when you use weighted values for the metrics.

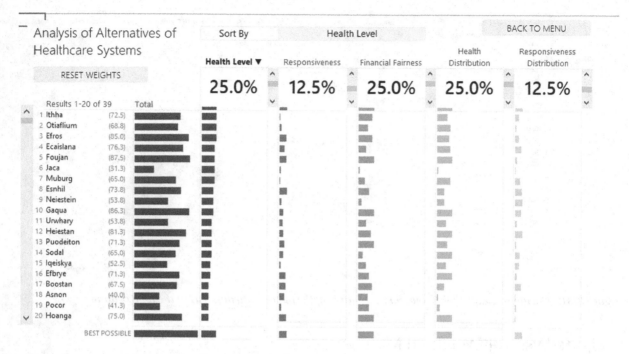

Figure 9-33. *Using weighted values instead of raw scores*

Your ability to compare values is much harder now. This is because each metric now has a different base against which to compare a best possible score. Consider country Efros, which is ranked in the third position in Figure 9-32. It's performance in Responsiveness and Financial Fairness is, in fact, the same. But you wouldn't glean this immediately since the representation in Responsiveness is half that of Financial Fairness. Switching back to raw values shows they are the same (Figure 9-34).

Figure 9-34. *Responsivness and Financial Fairness result in the same score for Efros*

Generally, we intuitively understand the concept of weighted models, especially when presented visually, as is the case here. In fact, this type of data visualization helps you mitigate your own bias. One common phenomenon, which I've experienced in my professional career, is the assumption that high performance in one (or two) metrics will strongly compensate for shortcomings in the rest.

In my past, I delivered a similar tool to an organization that wanted to gain insight into the performance of its different projects. Management's assumption was that because two metrics had performed well, the project should have ranked in the first or second spot. However, when presented with the tool above, they realized these two metrics were not given high weights. Indeed, you can see an example of this in Figure 9-35.

Figure 9-35. *The top four performing countries by weight*

Heiestan, for instance, ranks very well in Responsiveness Distribution. But that only makes up 12.5% of the overall score. Similarly, the top performer, Foujan, doesn't do well in Responsiveness Distribution, but that deficiency is easily offset by a strong performance in more heavily weighted metrics.

Color Choices

I chose blue as my predominant color. That choice isn't so important; I happen to like blue as color. (And it seems to go well with Excel's standard grey.) Whatever color choice you go with, it should be consistent, simple, and not overwhelming. Here, your metrics make up the total score. Varying the hue of the original blue color gives the sense of this part-to-whole relationship while similarly establishing that these metrics exist as their own measures.

Excel's color choices have gotten significantly better in terms of varying hue. But I've found for more than three metrics, the difference in color sometimes feels too strong. So for this decision support tool, I deferred my color choices to the ColorBrewer tool (www.colorbrewer2.org) shown in Figure 9-36. With this tool, you can define what type of data you're looking at and how many data classes you have. In my case, I chose to use a sequential hue with given data classes (based on my five metrics). ColorBrewer is a great tool to help you decide on a color palette for your work. It can even suggest color-safe alternatives that will not cause issues for those with color blindness.

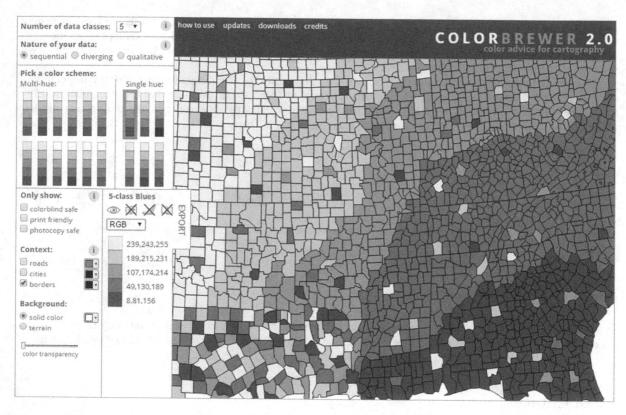

Figure 9-36. *The ColorBrewer tool (www.colorbrewer2.org)*

Notice in Figure 9-36, there is a dropdown box displaying RGB. By default, this dropdown box will display the Hex code color values often used for web development. However, to insert a custom color into Excel, you need to get the Red, Green, and Blue (RGB) code values. So you'll need to adjust that dropdown to say RGB.

Once you have the colors you like, you can simply type each color directly into Excel's color picker. Excel will remember these colors for later. An easy way to add these colors is to select an empty cell and then click the dropdown button next to the Fill Color icon in the Font group on the Home tab. From there, select More Colors and then click the Custom tab in the Colors dialog box that appears. You can now use those RGB code values to type in the custom color, as I have in Figure 9-37.

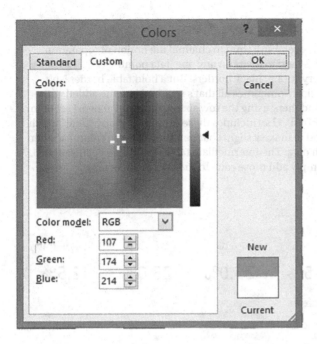

Figure 9-37. The Colors dialog box where you can add custom colors to the spreadsheet

Once complete, the color will be accessible from the recent colors section in the dropdown next to the Fill Color icon (Figure 9-38).

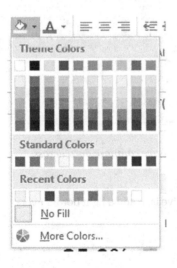

Figure 9-38. The Fill Color dropdown shows the custom colors that have been recently added to the spreadsheet

Data Spacing

I've similarly kept the table borders to a minimum. Here, however, I still want to channel the notion of separation. Sometimes when there's too much data bunched together, it's hard to focus on any one data point.

Most folks, when faced with this problem, will create very strong, black borders. But a bold table border isn't needed here, and it would surely overwhelm more than it helps. Sometimes all that's required is some added white space. In Figure 9-39, I inserted a new row every five rows, and then, using the row sizing trick from above, I set them all to be a consistent size. (The project file `Chapter9WizardFinal.xlsm` includes these extra rows as my "final" touch.) There is one unfortunate drawback to this method: if you had to make a slight change to any of these columns, when you drag down from the top, the extra rows would fill in with data. The intermediate table would also be misaligned, having no spaces in it. One way around this problem is to simply add those rows to the intermediate table.

Figure 9-39. *Added white space every five rows creates some seperation in our minds as we compare data across the spreadsheet*

But I'm also not entirely against using borders. Another equally effective alternative is to add a light border every five metrics or so. Figure 9-40 shows an example of this.

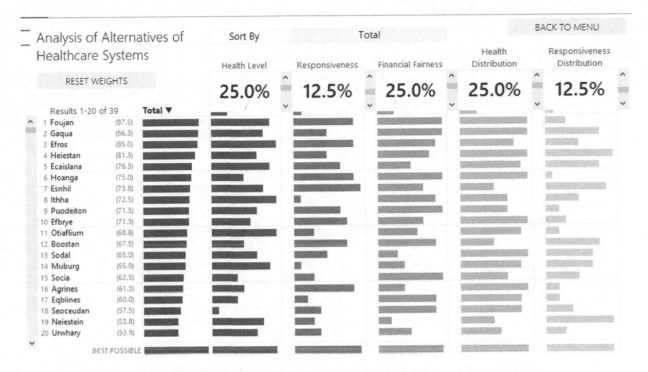

Figure 9-40. *Adding a slight border every five rows makes everything feel slightly less scrunched together*

Ultimately, the decision is up to you. There are many good ways (and innumerable terrible ways) you can help the user better interpret and contextualize visualized data. Here you're trying to optimize understanding of metric performance and importance: performance in terms of individual scores and importance in terms of weight. You should create your spreadsheet in a way that helps everyone understand both.

The Last Word

In this chapter, you perfected the link between your intermediate table and the visual layer. This included making properly sized scroll bars and developing in-cell bar charts. You saw that many of the items used in this spreadsheet application were not all that new. Instead, they were natural extensions of components built previously in this book. Finally, you saw there's a lot you can do with both code and formulas. Just as you attempt to achieve visual balance in your data displays, so too should you attempt to find the correct balance of formulas and VBA. Pursuing this balance is part of the journey.

But now that journey as come to an end. My hope with this book is that you learned how to do amazing things with Excel. Many in the industry would argue we should no longer use Excel. Their experience with the spreadsheet software is one of sluggishness, unpredictability, and application crashes. However, this book has showed that complex products can be created in Excel that are fast, predictable, and safe.

Going forward, hopefully you'll see how concepts in this book can be applied to your own work as reusable components. It might take creativity on your part to apply these examples, but I have faith in your ability to do so. Remember, the most important skill when building something truly amazing in Excel can't be found in this or any other book. Creativity comes from within. If you choose to be never satisfied with perceived limits, and have a continued thirst to learn new things, there's no telling what you can accomplish.

Now go, and create.

Index

191

Get the eBook for only $10!

Now you can take the weightless companion with you anywhere, anytime. Your purchase of this book entitles you to 3 electronic versions for only $10.

This Apress title will prove so indispensible that you'll want to carry it with you everywhere, which is why we are offering the eBook in 3 formats for only $10 if you have already purchased the print book.

Convenient and fully searchable, the PDF version enables you to easily find and copy code—or perform examples by quickly toggling between instructions and applications. The MOBI format is ideal for your Kindle, while the ePUB can be utilized on a variety of mobile devices.

Go to www.apress.com/promo/tendollars to purchase your companion eBook.

Apress®
THE EXPERT'S VOICE™